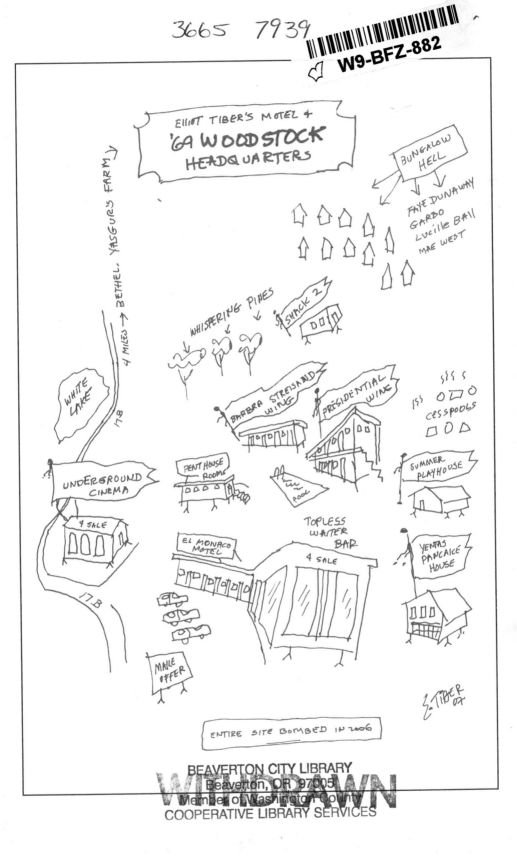

Taking Woodstock

Elliot Tiber
With Tom Monte

SQUAREONE
PUBLISHERS

You're probably thinking: Why should a nonfiction book have a disclaimer? I'll tell you why. Just in case I find myself on *Oprah,* I don't want to be falsely *outed* in front of millions of people about exaggerating or twisting things around. As you'll read, I was already outed in Chapter 8 by my mother—and that was enough. So to be as honest as I can, here's what I did: I changed a number of people's names who may still be alive. I didn't like them then, so why should I give them any credit now? For them, let me say that any resemblance to these actual Nazi bastards—oops, I mean, persons—dead or alive (or those who don't know they're dead) is coincidental. I also changed two settings because my publisher kvetched it would be less graphic and funnier, and would reduce the chances of a lawsuit. The fact is the stuff that happened, *happened.* Now that the world knows, I no longer fear Oprah.

COVER DESIGNER: Jeannie Tudor

IN-HOUSE EDITOR: Joanne Abrams

TYPESETTER: Gary A. Rosenberg

Square One Publishers

115 Herricks Road

Garden City Park, NY 11040

(516) 535-2010 • (877) 900-BOOK

www.squareonepublishers.com

Library of Congress Cataloging-in-Publication Data
Tiber, Elliot, 1935-
Taking Woodstock : a true story of a riot, a concert, and a life / Elliot Tiber ; with Tom Monte.
p. cm.
ISBN-10: 0-7570-0293-5
ISBN-13: 978-0-7570-0293-9
1. Tiber, Elliot, 1935- 2. Gay men—New York (State)—Biography. 3. Woodstock Festival. I. Monte, Tom. II. Title.

HQ75.8.T53T53 2007
306.76'62092—dc22
[B]

2007018502

Printed in the United States of America

10   9   8   7   6   5   4   3   2   1

Contents

This book is dedicated to Michael Lang,
producer of the 1969 Woodstock Music
and Arts Festival at White Lake, Bethel, New York.

Michael, you gave me an entire new life
and opened up a world filled with
dreams and self-esteem.
You have my lifelong heartfelt thanks.

This book is also dedicated
to the memory of Andre Ernotte.
A director. A poet. A writer.
An artist. A mensch.
My lover and best friend.

Acknowledgments

Thanks to all of you who have been so supportive and loving over the years:

Alyce Finell

Joan and Lydia Wilen

Neal Burstein, Esq.

Jack Blumkin, CPA

Robin and Steve Kaufman

Manhattan Plaza

Steve Corvi

Haig Palanjian

Helen Hanft

Joe Sidek (Penang)

Todd Hoffman

Daniel Bohr

Christian Lang

Jon Gabrietta

Calvin Ki

Katharine Hepburn

Ingrid Bergman

Michael Moriarty

Molly Picon

Marlon Brando

Wally Cox

Tennessee Williams

Truman Capote

Sammy Davis, Jr.

Arlo Guthrie

Melanie

Virginia Graham	Richie Havens
David Schnitter	Queen Fabiola of Belgium
Marti Mabin	President Giscard D'Estaing
Rosi Rogic	John Roberts
Renee Teichberg Brisker and	Joel Rosenman
Yuri Brisker	Artie Kornfeld
Rachelle Teichberg Golden	Stan Goldstein
and Sam Golden	Annie Cordy
Roger Orcutt	Claude Lombard
Andre Bishop of Lincoln Center	Anny Duperey
RTB TV Brussels	Bernard Giraudeux
Editions Rossel of Belgium	Max Yasgur
CineVog Film of Paris	Lee Blumer
Life Magazine	Woodstock-Preservation Archives

Finally, I would like to express my heartfelt appreciation and thanks to the wonderful people at Square One Publishers who helped make this book possible: Rudy Shur, Joanne Abrams, and Anthony Pomes. And last but certainly not least, thanks go to Tom Monte, who helped make this book a reality.

1

Lost in White Lake

"Elli!"

There it was again. My momma, like a woman caught in a burning building, was screaming my name at the top of her lungs. She screamed so loud that I could hear her voice over the roar of the mower that I reluctantly pushed around the lawn. Her voice was coming from the office of the motel that we owned in White Lake, New York, a tiny lakeside village in the Catskill Mountains. I turned and looked at the office to see if there were any flames or billowing smoke. Nothing, of course. The crisis was probably no more life-threatening than a leaky faucet.

"Eliyahu!!!" Now she used my full name to tell me how serious things were. "Get over here. Your suffering momma needs you." Her voice was as penetrating as a knife.

I turned off the rusty old mower and walked to the office. My mother was standing behind our counter facing a short man in red shirt, mustard yellow Bermuda shorts, knee socks, and a little hat pushed down on his bald head. He was so angry that the rage radiated from his back.

"What's the problem, Ma?"

"This gentleman with his fancy Cadillac, he wants a refund," she said, her right hand hatcheting the air and then coming to rest on her chest, as if in expectation of an impending heart attack. "I told him, I said, 'No refunds.' I didn't walk here from Minsk in Russia in twenty-foot snow drifts with the cold potatoes in mine pocket and the Czar's soldiers running after me just so I should give a refund on your room, Mr. Fancy Gentleman who complains about mine sheets."

"The sheets are stained," he said, trying to control his rage. "And I found . . . pubic hairs on the bed, for Chrissake. The telephone doesn't work and there's no air conditioner—just a plastic box in the window."

It was all true, of course. For years, we didn't have a washing machine so my father, who was the motel's handyman and jack-of-all-trades, took the sheets down into the basement, piled them high, poured on some detergent, and hosed them down. Sometimes he didn't bother with the detergent. Then we hung them out to dry in the swampy lot behind the motel, where hundreds of pine trees were located, to give them that "pine fresh" scent.

When we finally did get a washing machine, Momma often refused to add detergent to the water as a way of saving money. Even now, she usually skipped the job of washing sheets altogether, and instead brushed off the hairs and ironed the sheets while they were still on the bed.

As for the phone and air conditioner, both were cosmetic. One day, a disgruntled employee from the telephone company showed up with a hundred phones and an old switchboard—probably from the 1940s—which he promised to install for us, illegally, for $500. My mother, ever the sharpie when it came to a bargain, made him a counteroffer.

"Darling phone man, you think I walked here from Minsk in 1914 at midnight with the raw potatoes in mine pockets so you could cheat me on phones? All we can pay is twelve dollars cash, plus a dozen beers and a big mother's portion of hot cholent," which was my mother's beef and potato stew. Then she sealed the deal by saying, "For all of that, we take it all!"

The guy shrugged his shoulders, dumped the mess of phones, lines, and switchboard in the office, took the money, and went for a drink. We were helpless without his expertise, of course, which meant that all we got for our twelve bucks was the illusion of having telephones. I had Pop put the phones in the rooms, which he did by installing them with staples and adhesive tape. Then we got some air conditioner covers and fitted them into the windows. Once that was done, I placed signs in the rooms and around the motel that said, "Pardon our appearance as we install telephones and air conditioning for your comfort."

These were some of the reasons we had our customers pay cash up front before they actually saw their rooms, and why I put a rather conspicuous sign on the office counter that said, "Cash only. No refunds." Whenever someone showed up and wanted to pay with a credit card, my mother sprang into action.

"Gentleman, listen on me. I am an old Jewish momma trying to buy some warm milk for her babies," she began. "I'll hold onto this plastic card until you get me cash from your wife. "

I couldn't be everywhere at once, which meant that my mother was often left one-on-one with potential paying customers—a nightmare from a business perspective, as well as a personal one, since I had to deal with the mess after she was done. Which brings me back to the man standing before me, who looked like he wanted to strangle both of us.

"There's no towel in the room, either," the man said.

"Oy, now with the towels. You want a towel," my mother said, "you pay extra. You want soap, you pay a dollar more. You think we're giving such things away? What, do I look like a Misses Rockafeller to you?"

"What kind of sham operation is this?" he asked, shaking his head. "I want my money back!"

I wanted to tell him that his money was already gone—that the minute he handed over his cash to my mother it slipped into some kind of cosmic gap in the space-time continuum, a black hole, the opening to which could be found in my mother's brassiere. Where it went from there was anyone's guess, but I tried not to think about such things. Still, no matter how many customers we had during any given month—even during the good months, which were painfully few—we never had the money to pay the mortgage and electric bill. The mysterious loss of money was all part of what I liked to call the Teichberg Curse, a malevolent scourge placed upon our family that ensured our ongoing financial ruin. This was one of the reasons I changed my name from Eliyahu Teichberg to Elliot Tiber, a pathetic and altogether ineffective attempt to distance myself from the family karma. Welcome to motel hell, I wanted to tell this man and anyone else who might be listening. But I spared him all the gory details and told him how things worked at our miserable hotel.

"The sign says, 'No refunds,'" I said flatly. "You pay your money and you get the room as is. That's the agreement here."

He slammed his hand down on the counter and stormed out of the office.

"Well, Mom, another satisfied customer," I said without looking at her. "You ever wonder why we don't get repeat business? There goes today's answer."

"You need a girlfriend!" my mother screamed. "When are you going to give me grandchildren?!" She followed me out the front door, her hand chopping the air for emphasis. "Elliot! Where are you going?"

"I'm going to the store. We need milk," I said.

I got into my black Buick convertible and drove onto Route 17B. Only when I saw our motel get smaller in my rearview mirror did I start to breathe normally again.

It was early June 1969, and the weather was about the only good thing you could find in White Lake, a tiny section of a small village called Bethel just ninety miles north of New York City. When we first arrived in White Lake in 1955, the village of Bethel had a volunteer fire department, one hostile plumber, twenty bars, and a population of some 2,500 souls—many of them, we later discovered, outright bigots. Not much had changed in the ensuing fourteen years.

The Catskills were widely referred to as the Borscht Belt, named for the beet soup favored by many Eastern European Jews. Jewish people began coming to the region at the outset of the twentieth century. They opened hotels, motels, and bungalow colonies where middle- and lower-income people—mostly Jewish New Yorkers—could escape the city heat. Eventually, big resorts were built, such as Grossinger's and The Concord, where many great comedians—including Sid Caesar, Danny Kaye, Mel Brooks, and Jerry Lewis—regularly performed.

The owners of the motels, bungalow colonies, and resorts created jobs and the region thrived for many years—that is, until the mid-1950s, when people found that they could travel to Florida or Santa Fe for the same price as a vacation in the Catskills. At that point, all the local businesses began to suffer. It was right around that time that my parents bought our motel, which we now called the El Monaco.

By the late 1960s, White Lake, like the entire Catskill resort region, was in the throes of an ever-accelerating downturn. All across Bethel, houses, motels, and old Victorian hotels were uniformly in decline. Porches rotted and window shutters hung off their hinges. Many residents let the ivy grow on the walls of their houses to conceal the peeling paint and bare, weathered wood below. The boat docks at White Lake were slowly sinking into the water. The so-called resorts were no better off. The Catskills were becoming famous for the mysterious fires that occurred after the first Tuesday in September, when the vacationers left for home. Tourist traffic declined and the place became deadly quiet. As business dried up, so did the jobs. People got laid off and the region fell on hard times. And guess who got the blame?

Every so often, I'd have a run-in with one of the locals who did not hesitate to share his rather low opinion of my ethnic and religious origins. One day, a young tough with red hair and a red, pimply face drove his tractor over to our motel to see if we needed our lawn mowed. The truth was, I couldn't afford to pay the few bucks he wanted for the job. I thanked him and said that the FBI would not permit mowing down the government's secret experimental nuclear vegetation growing on our grounds.

I was just trying to be friendly and share a laugh with him, but apparently he didn't get the joke.

"You fuckin' kike faggot! You fuckin' with me? I'll get you, you cocksucking fag Jewboy. I'll get you and your whoring mother, too!"

Did I say the wrong thing? Maybe he was a touch sensitive on the subject of secret government experiments. A few hours later, he drove his tractor into what I gleefully called the Presidential Wing of our motel. Pop replaced the broken wood paneling with some doors and we all agreed that the remodeling job was an improvement over the old design.

Most of the anti-Semites and displaced Nazis weren't violent—at least not until later that summer, when a lot of weird and unexpected events started taking place. Many were just as happy to express their displeasure at the existence of our motel, and the Teichberg family, in slyer terms.

There was a sandwich shop and bar in Bethel that I used to frequent for its great parmigiana heroes. The place was run by a guy named Bud, also known as Joe, who lived above his bar with two grown sons who made bricks look smart. One day, I entered Bud's place in the middle of the afternoon and found him surrounded by some of the local intelligentsia, all of them drunk and disheveled. Bud was holding court.

"I passed by your place at closing time last night," Bud was saying through a thin, malevolent smile, "and saw you had some mighty strange, big fat women coming out of your motel. Do you charge extra for big gals doing that dirty stuff in your motel rooms? The boys and me were wondering if you can ever get the bed sheets really clean after those kind of women use them. Me? I'd never rent rooms to no dirty lesbos!"

As Bud let forth these sharp-witted observations, the boys hung over their drinks, giggling and panting like hyenas waiting for their prey to make a wrong move.

"Two lame nuns, Bud," I told him. "Those women last night were both wounded in Korea taking care of our boys. Blinded by mortar shells, poor ladies. They drink to forget what they went through." The hyenas shut their mouths and looked at me, suddenly confused. "But hey," I continued, "if you think we shouldn't welcome heroines like those to our fair town, let's talk at the next Chamber of Commerce meeting."

By some bizarre twist of fate, I was president of the Bethel Chamber of Commerce. I had become a member to help attract more business to Bethel in general, and the El Monaco in particular. And given that I was the best educated member present when the vote for president was cast, I became the Chamber's leader. Go figure.

Driving along Route 17B, I had the impression that one of the local friendlies might toss a rock my way. But all such concerns disappeared as I drove onto my friend Max's farm.

Max was our milkman. He and his wife, Miriam, owned the prettiest stretch of rolling hills and little valley bowls in all of Sullivan County. He had studied real estate law at New York University, but moved upstate in the 1940s to start a dairy farm. Over the years, Max and Miriam had created one of the largest and most successful dairy productions in eastern New York, complete with a massive refrigeration complex and trucking lines that went all over the state, as well as northern Pennsylvania. The two ran a little shop on the farm that sold their dairy products and a few simple grocery items. Pipe-smoking, wise, and avuncular, Max was a prince and the only real friend I had among the locals. Every year,

I did my best to bring more people—and, therefore, more business—to White Lake by organizing a music and arts festival. I also put on plays at the theater that we built on our property out of a barn. Max provided free dairy products, such as yogurt and ice cream, for the audience. He also drove his little red truck around town and posted flyers in the local establishments, advertising the music and arts festival, or the play we might be putting on. Yet, he always insisted on paying for his tickets to the concerts and plays.

Often, I drove to Max's farm just to get away from the insanity of my motel and my parents—not to mention the fine people of White Lake. Now I moved around his store with a comforting familiarity, picking up containers of milk, yogurt, butter, jam, and other groceries. Meanwhile, Max and I shot the breeze.

"You holding your music festival this summer, Elliot?" Max asked.

"Yup," I said.

"Anybody special playing?"

"Just the usual gathering of struggling bands. Most of them are local," I said. "We'll probably deafen a few people and outrage a few more, but it'll be a music festival just the same."

"I'll be there," Max said. "You bring a lot to our town, Elliot. God knows we need something. Anything I can do to help, you let me know. Bring over any leaflets you have and I'll see that they get around town."

"Thanks, Max. I just hope we get a few people to show up this year," I said. The only people I could ever count on coming were Max, the Grossingers, and a few other owners of the bigger resorts.

"You keep doing what you're doing, Elliot," Max said. "Who knows? Word will spread and your festival may catch on. You may be surprised."

"Don't count on it, Max. Rumor has it that the mob used to bury the bodies in White Lake because they knew that Bethel is just another word for lost."

Max laughed as he punched the prices of my few items into his cash register.

"But thanks for the support, Max. My fantasies are all that keep me going these days." That, and the good-natured calm of my friend, Max Yasgur.

Truth was, I cherished a lot of fantasies, and those secrets closest to my heart could not be revealed to the ordinary folk of White Lake, or to much of the rest of the world, for that matter. But one fantasy did involve this joyless place, and that millstone I called a motel. I dreamed of creating a music festival that would bring people to Bethel, fill my motel, and show a profit so I could sell the thing to some rich fool. So far, we hadn't turned a profit in the fourteen years we owned the place, and thanks to the Teichberg Curse, my music and arts festivals were a bust. But some fantasies die hard, and for reasons that were an utter mystery to me, I still had hope.

2

The Teichberg Curse

I was born in Bensonhurst, a section of Brooklyn, New York, famous for its racism and cannolis. Bensonhurst, at least when I was growing up, was made up predominantly of guilt-ridden Italians and Jews. A lot of famous people from both ethnic groups emerged from its womb, including Danny DeVito, Elliott Gould, Larry King, and The Three Stooges. The Teichbergs were The Six Stooges—double the insanity.

My mother, having trekked through the Russian snows, arrived in New York in 1912. My father's parents had come to the city from Austria ten years before my mother. They settled in Borough Park, where my grandfather established a roofing business. Since he was a young child in Salzburg, my father had worked as my grandfather's assistant. When the time came for him to choose a profession in his newly adopted country, Pop's career was pretty much set in tar. Not all of his choices were a direct reflection of his parents, however. When my father and mother started dating, my grandmother—never known for her subtlety—gave my father some thoughtful advice. Loosely translated from Yiddish, she told him, "Get rid of that ignorant Russian slut." Not one to recognize good advice, he married her instead.

Like many immigrants, my parents distrusted banks. Instead, they stuffed their money into their mattress. So when the Depression hit and the banks collapsed, my parents were lying on a few thousand dollars—enough to buy a three-story, three-bedroom, one-bath house on Seventy-Third Street. They also purchased a four-story walk-up on Seventieth Street and Twentieth Avenue. On the bottom floor of that house, they opened a hardware and housewares store, where my mother's greed first reared its gargantuan green head.

There were no prices on anything in my parents' store, a flexible strategy that enabled my mother to set the price based on how much she thought the person could pay. Sometimes customers would call across the store to ask the price of some item they wanted. My mother would race over to the customer, use her psychic gift to instantaneously determine the customer's financial status, and then quote a price. "For you, darling, nineteen dollars and ninety-nine cents, and not a penny more! Special because I'm feeling very generous today." Momma's store was the original Wheel of Fortune.

At six o'clock every night—save Saturday, the only day the store was closed—my mother would ride her bicycle home to Seventy-Third Street. What a sight she was coming down the street— a small fullback perched on bent frame and straining tires, pedaling furiously. You could almost see the numbers whizzing around her head as she calculated the day's receipts.

Once home, Momma would set to work making dinner. Smoke and putrid fumes would soon fill the air, and at the center of the billowing clouds was the vague outline of Momma's cylindrical frame. Her specialty was grease—flavored with garlic. Tucked inside the grease were a few scraps of meat and vegetables, but the main dish was always a lumpy goop that she ladled onto plates with a motherly pride that barely concealed a wrath warning off potential critics.

My sister Goldie, twelve years my senior, gorged on my mother's food, as I did, which partly explains why both of us were overweight. It's amazing how good grease can taste when you have no basis for comparison. Rachelle, nine years older than me, and Renee, four years younger, picked around the food's edges as if it were some form of toxic waste. Not surprisingly, the two were always thin. The only thing that saved us from Momma's dangerous food was the supply of chocolate bars, candy, and doughnuts that each of us kept stashed away in our rooms. The treats—purchased by my father, who had a sweet tooth—also served as self-medication against my mother's harsh tongue.

"You're fat and stupid, Eliyahu," my mother regularly told me, using my original Hebrew name so she would be sure that I heard her. "Stupid, do you hear me? What's going to become of your poor mother?" she wailed. "Why do I put up with you? You're going to kill me, do you hear me?" At that point, I usually escaped the only way I could—by running upstairs to my room, where I kept my stash of doughnuts and chocolate bars.

After dinner, my mother and father would go back to the store and work until eleven in the evening, long after every soul had vanished from the streets. When I reached adolescence, I too went back to the store with them, sometimes working until midnight. When I wasn't working at the hardware store, I helped my father with his roofing business. I was never paid a cent for any of the work I did for my parents, but I was raised to believe that this was my lot in life.

My father's average workday was anywhere from twelve to sixteen hours long. After spending all day covering roofs with sheets of tar, he went home, ate dinner, grabbed a short nap—if he was lucky—and then went to work at the hardware and housewares circus. There, he did general maintenance, fixed irons and toasters, and made keys behind a cluttered counter that would eventually look just like the one at the El Monaco Motel.

My father—a simple, humble man—coped with his life by escaping from it as much as possible. He listened to the radio, bent over and lost in concentration as if it were the voice of God coming out of that box. He smoked continuously, and napped whenever possible—that is, until my mother wanted me punished for something. Momma's piercing voice would cut through his loud snoring like a buzz saw through a thick log. "Jaaaaaaaack!" she shrieked. "Come down here now. Maybe they'll behave for you!" When my father stormed down the stairs, he was already loosening his belt. My father had the build and strength of a man who had done manual labor all of his life. When he hit you, you usually rattled for an hour or two afterwards.

After I was beaten silly and had finished screaming my lungs out, I would be sent to bed without dinner—which, now that I think about it, wasn't such a terrible thing. But later, before she went back to the store, Momma would sneak a meal up to my room anyway. She would sit on the edge of my bed as I ate and make me promise—in a whisper, lest my father hear us—that I would be a good boy for the rest of my life.

This was the closest thing I ever got to a mother's love—those intimate moments after the punishment, the welts still fresh on my body, when she served me her stew. She actually succeeded in doubling my guilt, as only she could. On one hand, she made it clear that I had wronged her—a grievous crime against nature and God. On the other, she drew me into some kind of bizarre conspiracy against my father. He had punished me—at her bidding, no less—but now Momma and I were friends and Pop was the outsider, the bad guy. He was left out of our intimate moment. Deep down, I knew that something was wrong here, and I was aware of a vague guilt. Heck, I was just a little kid, hungry for love and food. But in our house, neither one tasted good.

My mother's psychic powers were not limited to divining the money in a customer's purse. She also got regular messages from the dead—or at least from one dead person, her father, who had been a rabbi. When I was four years old, my mother received telepathic instructions from her father to send me to Yeshiva. The rabbi declared that it was my purpose to become a rabbi, too, so that I could bring *nochas* (Yiddish for "pleasure") to my long-suffering mother. Thus, at the tender age of four—she had to lie about my age to get me into the school—I was packed off and sent to Yeshiva.

It was a living hell—eight hours a day studying an ancient language and Talmudic laws governing cows that wander onto your front yard. True, wandering cows weren't a big problem in Brooklyn, but still, I had to know what to do if a cow *did* wander in. Fear permeated the entire deal—fear of Moses and all of his laws, which you couldn't help but break, and fear of that "jealous" and "vengeful" God, who regularly got pissed off and sent plagues upon fat little Yeshiva students who denied His existence. At the age of five, I announced my atheism, much to the chagrin of the rabbis who taught me.

But Moses had the last laugh. Yeshiva, it turned out, was also a social nightmare. Rather than making me feel a part of something larger than myself, the school deepened my isolation. In the first place, I had been taken away from my neighborhood and sent to a private Jewish institution populated by rich kids whose parents drove them to school in Cadillacs. My father brought me to school in his green Ford pickup truck. Of course, I was teased for being fat, ugly, and poor, and for the fact that my father was covered in tar when he picked me up after school each day.

Once I got home, it was no better. Because I didn't attend public school, I had no bond with the neighborhood kids, some of whom ridiculed me for going to Yeshiva. To make matters worse, I liked classical music, which put me completely out of step with the rest of my generation. I was a nerd before the word even existed.

My only outlets were drawing and painting, and ironically, the hardware store provided me with many opportunities to do both. There, I was allowed to fashion decorative displays in our store's windows. I emptied the window and selected and arranged products in an appealing array. I then painted wild backdrops and witty signs, and sometimes made papier-mâché figures. When I asked Momma if I could buy some balloons or crepe paper to highlight my designs, she reminded me (yet again) of that long walk through the twenty-foot snows of Russia with the Czar's soldiers at her back. "What do I look like, Eliyahu? The Czarina?"

When the balloons were refused, I took some high-gloss electric pink paint and created murals and funny cartoons to give the window some humor and style. Painting and designing allowed me to escape the insanity and isolation of my own world for a life that was beautiful, harmonious, and orderly. Ordinary objects—pots and pans, lights, ladders, and tool belts—became elements of art. Objects that had no obvious relationship with each other suddenly seemed connected when they were arranged in just the right way.

When a window was finished, I would ask my parents to come over and have a look. Pop shrugged his shoulders. Momma, ever suspicious of theft, inspected the materials to make sure I hadn't taken anything essential from the store. "I don't want you to be wasting nails, Eliyahu. Do you hear me?" The only time I ever saw her smile was when the day's receipts were good.

In the summers, I worked with my father patching roofs all over Brooklyn. I would schlep tarpaper and supplies up tall ladders to the tops of buildings. Ladders and heights scared the tar out of me. I would cling to the rungs for dear life, trying desperately not to look down, while at the same time carrying a bucket of tar or a bundle of tarpaper. Once on the roof, my father and I would spread the paper and wet tar over the rooftop, all the while baking in the summer sun. We weren't building the pyramids, but it sure seemed like slave labor to me.

Yet what strange bonds are forged between father and son who work together, mostly in silence. As I watched my father labor in the sun and heat, I tried to do the same, not just to follow his example, but to gain his love. I imagined that he felt some hint of what I was feeling—that we were joined, not just in the common goal of getting the job done quickly and correctly, but in the heart, too. We were comrades in our shared struggle to survive my mother's daily assaults.

Of course, working in the roofing business made me seem all the more weird to the few friends I had in the neighborhood. They spent at least part of their summers in the Catskills and came home with wonderful stories of boating, fishing, swimming, and hiking in the woods. When they asked me what I did during the summer, I looked down at my blackened hands and said, "Oh, nothing much. I was just working with my father." And to this day, I still love the smell of fresh tar.

☮   ☮   ☮

Because I started first grade when I was four, I was ready for college at the age of sixteen. I had my heart set on the Pratt school of art and design in New York. Tuition was five hundred dollars, which I had saved from my bar mitzvah and was all too happy to shell out to escape Seventy-Third Street. But fate, which is to say my mother, had other plans. My sister Goldie was getting married and gifts had to be given. A chartreuse, kidney-shaped sectional sofa, which was the rage at the time, cost about two hundred dollars. She had to have an engagement party, which was another two hundred, and, of course, a wedding dress for another hundred or so.

"I am going to borrow five hundred dollars from you, Eliyahu," my mother told me.

"Do I have a choice?" I asked weakly.

"What's a matter with you, you don't trust your mother? What kind of a son are you? I ran through the Russian snow with the Czar's soldiers trying to cut me in two so I could bring you into the world, and you want to deprive your mother of her only joy in life—to give her daughter a wedding!"

That was it—I knew the money was gone. I couldn't stop the tears from welling up in my eyes and running down my face. My one and only escape from Bensonhurst was being torn from my chubby little fingers. "Are you really going to pay me back, Mom?" I asked. "I need that money for college."

"Jaaaaaaaack!" my mother screamed. "Get down here. Your son is breaking his mother's heart!" I could hear my father's belt coming off as he ran down the stairs.

When the time came for me to send in my five hundred dollar tuition payment to Pratt, Momma announced that she couldn't pay me back because she needed the money for the mortgage and she had to buy my sister Rachelle some new dresses. "How can Rachelle meet some nice Jewish husband wearing Goldie's old kitchen-curtain dresses?" she asked over my tears. And just like that, my dream of going to Pratt was gone.

Fortunately, fate offered an alternate escape route. The city and state of New York covered the costs of a college education for its needy residents. At the time, Hunter College—long a women's school—was in financial trouble. In order to stay in business, the administration decided to have a disaster sale. They would increase enrollment, and thus qualify for needed city and state funds, by admitting male students with bad grades and no money. I fit the profile perfectly.

Hunter was not my first alternate choice. After Pratt, I would have preferred to go to Brooklyn College, where the avant-garde of modern art was teaching, but Brooklyn had high standards and only the smart kids with good grades could get in. So it was either Hunter or nothing. But after my freshman year, my grades were good enough to get into Brooklyn, which was where I studied with and befriended some of the masters of modern art—Mark Rothko, Ad Reinhardt, Jimmy Ernst, and Kurt Seligman. Although all of them would eventually be regarded as superstars in the art world, they were still unknown and broke when I studied with them.

Mark Rothko, whose paintings now hang in the Guggenheim, the National Gallery of Art, the Metropolitan Museum of Art, the Museum of Modern Art, and London's famed Tate Gallery, became both my mentor and my friend. In a way, he adopted me as one of his protégés. He worked with me long after classes were finished. "Your pen and ink drawings show an artist's sensitivity," he told me one day. "I will teach you the language of ink, and later the paints."

Rothko was known for his use of color, which communicated the raw emotions that he felt and that he wanted to evoke from those who viewed his paintings. His huge murals and abstract forms often brought his admirers to tears. Many claimed to have religious experiences while gazing at his work, and he said that those who felt such emotions were sharing in the experience he had when he was painting.

Rothko rejected every label the art world tried to place on him, including colorist and abstract artist. "I'm not interested in the relationship between form and color," he used to say. "The only thing I care about is the expression of man's basic emotions—tragedy, ecstasy, and destiny."

When we were friends, he was broke most of the time. I used to share my cigarettes and bring him sandwiches and an occasional bottle of wine. He had big, round eyes, soulful and sad, and a little black mustache that, when his expression was just right, brought to mind a young Groucho Marx. One day, after we had eaten lunch and were smoking, Mark said to me, "Ignore your Russian mother. I am also Russian," his original name was Marcus Rothkowitz, "so I know what I am talking about. Erase everything she ever told you. She is wrong about everything. Move out into your own studio. Tell her to become a rabbi, not you."

Sometimes he would allow me to hang out in his studio and watch him work. I witnessed his struggle to find form and color to express the hidden passions and existential pain that is the human condition. It was obvious that the man was a genius. And, in truth, I was honored to be in his company.

"You have a genuine artistic talent and a poet's soul," he told me one day. I treasured those words all my life. I was an artist—that much I knew. But having Mark Rothko respect my work and encourage me was like being blessed by a king. And indeed, I was so deeply drawn into his world, and the world of art, that I knew, if only unconsciously, that I was on the threshold of some kind of initiation. Art, like a vast corridor whose door had now mysteriously opened, was calling me in. I looked down that corridor, and then at Mark, and I wondered if I wasn't looking at my own fate—to be dirt-poor, unrecognized, and overcome by my own dark passions.

Mark wasn't only broke; he was frequently despondent and depressed. Eventually, he committed suicide by cutting his wrists. Other artists I knew and admired were plagued by that same poverty and darkness. Ad Reinhardt, another of my teachers and mentors, was a heavy drinker and chronically depressed. I remember the day I stood with him in his studio and watched him cry his eyes out because he couldn't get the black paint intense enough in one of his paintings. He was a great man and a great artist, but much of the time he was a total wreck. More than once I took long walks with Kurt Seligman and listened to him rant and rave about his dire financial straits and the tragic depths to which his life had fallen. He was miserable.

These men were high priests who gave their lives to serve the only god they knew and worshipped—art. Their reward was to produce great works that, at the time I knew them, went largely unappreciated and unnoticed. The price they paid to produce such art was inordinately high; they sacrificed any chance at ordinary happiness and love. No doubt, their anguish was part of what fueled their art. But the depths of their passion, pain, and poverty terrified me. By observing them up close, I was forced to answer the single most important question facing every young artist: Am I willing to give everything I have, and everything that I am, to the service of art, without any guarantee of reward or recognition? For me, the question was complicated by the fact that I was a lot like them in temperament. My sanity, such as it was, hung by a pretty thin thread. And like them, I was beset by demons. Look at what I had come from! If I was sucked into art's long dark corridor, as they had been, I would turn out as miserable as they were. And they were broke to boot.

No, I told myself. I need to hang on to the precious few marbles I have left. I also need an income that's more secure and dependable. I cannot live as they do—broke and desperately unhappy. I had spent my entire childhood there, and I needed to escape all that.

My senior year, I transferred back to Hunter College because I had been told that a degree from Hunter looked better on a job application than one from Brooklyn College. Before I left, Mark Rothko gave me five original pen and ink drawings. It was a gift straight from the heart and I was thrilled. I wrapped the drawings carefully and placed them in my room at home for safekeeping.

Of course, years later, Rothko was recognized throughout the world; his works were sold for great fortunes. In fact, one of Rothko's greatest masterpieces, "White Center," sold for seventy-three million dollars—a record price for any postwar painting sold at auction in the United States.

A few years after Rothko gave me those pen and ink drawings, I went looking for them in my room. They were gone. Frantic, I asked my mother about the missing pieces. "Oh," she said, "I threw those away along with all that other trashy art in your room."

Since she could never comprehend the emotional value of a painting, I explained my loss in the only terms I felt she would understand. "Those pieces were worth more than fifty thousand dollars, Momma," I told her.

"What a liar you are," she retorted. "They was nothing—just somebody's *mishegas*."

I was furious, but I knew that there was nothing I could do. My mother was oblivious to any point of view other than her own. In my room, I stuffed myself silly with chocolate. Milton Hershey was my patron saint.

I graduated from Hunter with honors, with a BFA in fine art and applied art and design. My first job was as a display designer and decorator at the swanky W. & J. Sloane on Fifth Avenue in Manhattan. Sloane's was a fine furniture emporium, strictly for the well-heeled. Who knew what fine furniture was? Not me. On top of that, I never dreamed that my portfolio could compete with those of the Pratt graduates. I was shocked when Walter Bahno, the director of Sloane's display department, offered me the job.

In my spare time, I painted murals in some of Manhattan's most expensive apartments. My paintings were also displayed in galleries and sold. My life had finally begun. I was making a very good living. And more important, I was free and ready to discover and express all that I was.

And yet, the inexplicable obligation I felt to my parents could override my desire to break away. The Teichberg Curse was a powerful force. Or maybe I had just inhaled too many tar fumes.

❥   ❥   ❥

It all began innocently enough. In the summer of 1955, while I was still in college, my parents finally decided to take a vacation in the Catskills. We all landed at Pauline's Rooming House in White Lake, New York, and stayed in her hot and musty attic. My parents, sisters, and I loved it. It was like falling into paradise, which, of course, got my mother thinking. There, in that cramped rooming house, as she furtively looked around Pauline's twenty rooms—all of them rented—my mother silently ran the numbers and saw the future. "Now *this* is a business," she said. "If we buy a house out here and get rid of the hardware store, then we could really make a fortune and live like this full-time!"

My father seemed to come to life, he liked the idea so much. Caught up in the moment, even I was excited.

Just down the road was an old, dilapidated Victorian rooming house for sale. The place was falling down, but my mother called it *beshert* ("destiny"—a sign from Guess Who). Had she walked around the block, she would have discovered that virtually the entire town was for sale, and most of it for a lot less. But, unfortunately, she didn't; and after all, a sign's a sign. She sold the hardware and housewares store, bought the rooming house, and turned the house's six rooms into nine. That done, the family moved to White Lake and waited for the season to begin.

That first summer, the place was sold out every night. We were ecstatic. The Teichbergs had struck gold. Soon, money was going to start sprouting from the trees, we thought. It was then that Momma's green demon started whispering in her ear again: Why not buy the house next door and turn both properties into a motel? Soon we had twelve more rooms and a building going up. My parents, of course, had no idea what a motel was. They had no business plan. They simply knew how to buy and build—when all of the other property owners were looking to sell and run. The following season, they bought a bungalow colony with a casino and expanded the motel to more than twenty rooms and several cottages.

As any good businessperson knows, you can grow too fast and go too far. There's a line that shouldn't be crossed, and my parents were about two hundred miles beyond it. Suddenly, there wasn't enough tourist traffic in White Lake to fill all the rooms they had purchased or built. Cash flow was reduced to a trickle. The mortgage was becoming difficult to pay each month, as were most of the other bills. The place started to sink deeper into debt. To make matters worse, my folks had no social skills to attract those tourists who *were* still coming to White Lake.

My father was the motel operator. This was how he would normally answer the phone: "Hello? What's this? Why you calling? What you want? If you got children, don't come here. We don't rent to children. They ruin mattresses, make noise. If you got kids, then we got no vacancy!"

By this time, I was out of college and working in Manhattan. My life had been launched and the stars were the limit, as far as I was concerned. As my fortunes rose, my parents' were sinking fast. When it became apparent that they were going to lose everything—their life savings, their only means of income, and the molecular traces of sanity they had left—they asked me to manage the motel for them.

With hindsight, I can see the moment so clearly, the not-so-subtle manipulation that dragged me into their nightmare—my father's contrite, slumped shoulders, head turned down, asking for my help; my mother, suddenly aware of and grateful for my instinct for managing a motel (who knew I had such a gift?). And then those few magical words that would trigger my subliminal programming—the guilt that Momma had taken years to cultivate for a moment such as this: "Oy, what will become of us if you don't help us, Eliyahu? Where are we to go?"

It wasn't just guilt that gripped my insides, however. Finally, I had a chance to prove myself worthy in my parents' eyes. Finally, I would have the two things that I had yearned for my entire life— their love and appreciation. For years, even as I tried to establish an independent life doing what I loved best, I had longed for their approval. Here was my chance to win it.

"Okay," I told them. We made an arrangement. I would stay in New York City during the week and continue my painting, and on weekends I would come to White Lake and manage the motel. Somewhere, Moses was laughing his head off.

When I told my plan to my sister Goldie, she was aghast.

"Get away from them, Elliot," she advised me. "Don't do it. Don't throw your life away on them and their stupid motel. Save yourself now. That motel will never work out."

Of course, her words proved all too prophetic, but I was too blind see the obvious. Besides, I still loved the smell of fresh tar.

3

My
"Other" Life

I stood in the shadows near the bar, leaning against the cigarette machine, chain-smoking and occasionally taking tokes on joints offered by hungry suitors. All three floors of The Mine Shaft, a sex club on Little Twelfth Street in Greenwich Village, were packed that night. I, however, was fixated on a single pair of eyes—aggressive, angry, and hungry for prey—that kept looking back at me. The object of my desire was tall, lean, and dressed from head to toe in tight black leather. Handcuffs and a cat-o'-nine-tails hung from one side of the outfit, and a leather hood was slung over one shoulder. I was dressed in similar garb, but I wasn't nearly as self-assured. In my mind, I was fat and ugly. Photographs taken of me at the time tell a somewhat different story, but it's the story inside your head that counts. As far as I was concerned, there was nothing about me that would attract someone with eyes as beautiful, if a bit terrifying, as those that devoured me from across the room that night.

Like a lion suddenly roused from its torpor and ready for dinner, my predator slowly moved toward me. He gave me an angry, malevolent stare and then punched me hard in the stomach. It was love at first smite. He then began his courting ritual by leading me to the center of the room, where he made me the object of foreplay for about a hundred men, all dressed as cops, state troopers, or in one case, a Nazi officer.

When I was a kid, the only attention I received came in the form of rejection. Here, suddenly, were dozens of men who wanted me. That was the beauty of the New York gay sex bars: Everyone wanted everyone else, even me. In many ways, I was the prototypical gay man, only more so. After being suppressed by every quarter of society, save our own, gay men unleashed their pent-up sexual desires and desperate need for acceptance in the sex bars and bathhouses of New York. What was hidden from our families and coworkers exploded into the open at places like The Mine Shaft. I felt uglier and more repulsive than most, which made any form of acceptance an instant aphrodisiac. My current situation—having dozens of men fondle, grope, grab, and pinch me in the center of the large, dimly lit room—was the fulfillment of one of my better sex dreams.

When the lion had witnessed enough, he walked over, pushed away the men who circled me, and spoke words of sweet poetry: "Clean yourself up, you fucking kike. You smell like a fucking toilet." I fairly swooned. Outside, he hailed a cab and took me back to "his place," which was a huge loft in SoHo.

I was made compliant by too much weed and too many THC pills, but the sight of his apartment shook me out of my intoxication. Hanging from one wall was an enormous Nazi flag, perhaps thirty feet wide and twenty feet tall. Here and there, long knives and sabers were on display. I preferred my sex play as ritualized sadomasochism. A few good slaps, punches, and kicks were essential, but stabbings and real blood were a definite turnoff. Something told me that my angry new friend might not observe the same limits.

"Hey, I don't feel too good, boss," I said. "I want to go."

"You're not going anywhere," he said. And with that, he whipped out a pair of handcuffs and slapped them on my wrists. He then threw a leather hood over my head and cuffed me to the bed. I was excited and terrified all at once, which made the sex all the more thrilling. We went at it for the rest of the night and the better part of the next day, until drugs and exhaustion finally consumed us.

After we had slept off our respective sex- and drug-induced stupors, I climbed out of bed and looked around his apartment. Had I not been blinded the night before by drugs, desire, and fear—of swastikas, in particular—I might have noticed that the walls were covered with the most amazing black-and-white photographs I had ever seen. These were certainly not your typical images. The men and women were caught in mesmerizing erotic poses, many blatantly sadomasochistic, and most of them very much on the edge. I recognized one of the subjects in the gallery of faces—the Greenwich Village singer, songwriter, and eventual punk rock icon Patti Smith.

Several of my hostile host's portraits were hung from the walls. A few posters for photographic exhibitions were framed and hung, as well. At the bottom of each poster was a single name: Robert Mapplethorpe. I didn't know anything about photography and the name didn't ring any bells.

"What do you do, boss?"

"I'm a photographer."

"So . . . you're Robert," I said.

"Yeah," he said. And with that, he slid a big partition from the wall, opening up another room that contained fifty feet of wooden bins, each of which was filled with photographs. I looked through the stacks and was awestruck. Without any doubt, I realized that Robert Mapplethorpe was some kind of genius. The incredible beauty and mind-altering point of view overwhelmed me. Many of the pictures were of flowers, each placed in a small vase and cast in light that was delicate, tender, and revealing. As for the people in the pictures, most were nude. Each photograph seemed to reveal the person's soul—this one strong, armored, warrior-like; that one utterly exposed, vulnerable, and terrified. Many of the photos caught men engaged in sex, and these portraits were very liberating and ultimately revolutionary. They depicted sex acts that homosexuals performed every day, but were denied by the larger society, just as gays themselves were denied. Mapplethorpe pulled homosexual sex—and, by extension, the very lives of gays—out of the closet and broadcast it to the world. Each photo was a statement of undeniable courage, a steadfast refusal to be marginalized or denied. Clearly, Robert was the kind of artist who shook the world, altering perceptions and challenging long-held beliefs with a single photograph.

Finally, he interrupted my reverie.

"I want to take your picture," he said.

"You do? Why?" I asked.

"I want to pose you in a Gestapo uniform."

"I don't think so, boss," I said.

"You'll do it," he said, his voice hard like granite.

We were not what you would call a match made in heaven.

"Maybe you'd like to come to White Lake with me some weekend," I suggested.

"I don't know where White Lake is," he said in a low, dismissive voice.

"It's upstate, just a couple of hours north on the New York State Thruway. We own a motel—nothing fancy, but it's private."

"You're not understanding me," he said. "I've got other plans, and they don't include becoming pals. I don't want to know anything about your fucking motel or the rest of your life. You ain't even my type." And so our dance began and ended.

Months later, I saw articles about him in *The Village Voice* and *SoHo News.* He was fighting the censorship of his photographs. After that, I stopped in at a downtown gallery that was exhibiting his work. When he saw me walk in, he looked at me as if he had never seen me before.

That pretty much summed up my sexual history. People with whom I had sex always pretended that they didn't know me when they saw me in the light of day. It had been that way ever since I was a kid.

❧   ❧   ❧

When I was eleven years old, I began sneaking out of my house during the day—sometimes at night—to go to the movies. I took the subway from Brooklyn to Manhattan's Times Square, where there were dozens of all-day-and-night movie theaters. I was tall for my age and easily passed for sixteen—not that anyone seemed to care. I asked for a ticket, paid the clerk, and was admitted to the films I wanted to see—movies starring Laurel and Hardy, Abbott and Costello, the Marx Brothers, Betty Grable, and Carmen Miranda.

During the 1940s and '50s, the theaters in Times Square were large, ornate palaces—originally used for plays, but later, for films. These movie houses had enormous balconies, or mezzanines, that could seat a couple of hundred people. Along the walls, about midway between the floor and the ceiling, could be found elaborate boxed seats. The walls and balconies were decorated in gold leaf, embossed lions heads, and other forms of ornamentation. The silver screen was enormous—a great white wall, two or three times the size of many of today's screens. Every ticket got you a double feature, as well as some news and a cartoon. You could spend the better part of a day or night watching movies and cartoons.

One night, a kid from my neighborhood named Frank, who was just two years my senior, sat down in the seat next to me. He didn't acknowledge me, but looked directly at the screen. I thought nothing of it and continued to watch the movie. Soon, I became vaguely aware that Frank's shoulder had inched closer to mine and his leg was rubbing up against my own. I ignored the advance until I realized that he had placed his hand on the inside of my leg. Then he removed his hand and seemed momentarily preoccupied with something. Suddenly, Frank turned to me and pointed a pocket-knife at my face.

"Elli, just sit there and keep your mouth shut," he whispered.

I froze. He put the knife away, resumed looking at the screen, and placed his hand on my crotch. Then he unzipped my pants and started fondling me. I sat there in terror. What's happening? What should I do? I knew this kid from my neighborhood. If I ran, he would beat me up when he saw me again. Soon, fear became mingled with a mysterious pleasure that I did not understand. I was a slow developer and had no knowledge of sex whatsoever. I had never even masturbated before, but Frank was masturbating me now and I was responding. Soon I climaxed and Frank got up and left without looking at me. The front of my pants was a little wet, but I didn't know why. My first thought was that I might be bleeding, which terrified me. I must have sat there for an hour in utter shock and confusion, not knowing what to do. Finally, an usherette appeared and shined her flashlight into my face. From behind her, I heard my father's voice say, "What are you doing here, Elli? Your mother, she's *meshugge* with worry. Where is mine son, she's wanting to know?"

He took me home, hit me with the belt, and sent me to bed. In my room, I undressed and found that there was no blood in my pants. I exhaled a long breath of relief. I sneaked downstairs to the basement. We had one of those old front-loading coal furnaces. I opened the door and threw my pants and underwear into the fire. Then I sneaked back upstairs, got into the shower, and, afterwards, went to sleep.

A few days later, one of my classmates at school asked our health teacher what the word "masturbation" meant. The teacher refused to answer, which immediately tipped me off that the word must be important. I went home that day and looked it up. *Okay,* I told myself. *That's what Frank did to me. Right. I get it. Says here that there are no ill effects. Nothing life-threatening. Well, that's good news!*

Now there was a new reason to go to the movies, and nothing was going to stop me, not even the threat of the belt.

In fact, Frank had opened my eyes to something that had been going on all around me without my realizing it. The movie theaters in Times Square were sex houses. Boys and boys, boys and men, girls and boys, and women and men were having sex all over the theater. The balconies were the preferred seats, because you could hide in the darkness. *The movies are where you go to get sex,* I realized. The revelation overwhelmed me with a strange and intense excitement. While Bud Abbott was slapping Lou Costello on the big screen, the patrons were happy-slapping each other in the aisles.

The next time I went to the movies, I sat in my seat, slouched down a little, and waited for someone to come by. It didn't take long. A man in a raincoat appeared. He took off the coat, sat down next to me, and threw the coat over his lap. Then he passed it over my lap, moved his hand under it, and started touching me. Revelation number two: There were crowds of raincoats all over the theater. Men were flashing boys and girls and performing all kinds of sex acts under their raincoats. The world was opening up to me, and I was like the proverbial kid in the sex store. I wanted all I could get. For the first time in my life, I felt desired.

As it turned out, this first raincoat and I became regulars. Every Friday night at seven-thirty, I'd show up at the theater and take my regular seat. Soon he would sit in the next seat and, without looking at me, throw his raincoat over my lap and go through his regular routine. This went on for a couple of months. But one night, a black man beat him to the spot and began fondling me. My regular suitor arrived late and instead of backing off, started fighting with the black man. The two were going at it in the aisle when my regular pulled a knife out of his pocket and chased off the black man.

Wow, what excitement! I could hardly imagine two men wanting me, much less fighting for me. I had never had such attention in all of my life. And then there was the touching. People were touching me with the intention of getting pleasure. And whether they intended it or not, they certainly gave me pleasure. My life to that point had been exactly the opposite experience. Every time I got touched in my house, it was associated with pain. But as I would soon learn, even pain could have its pleasures.

Later, in my teens, I moved on to other movie houses. One night at the Rialto, also in the Times Square area, a tall, well-dressed man in a suit sat down next to me—someone whom Momma would definitely call a "darling gentleman." He unzipped my pants and began punching my penis until it got rock hard. Then he began scratching me with his fingernails until I felt some blood trickle into my crotch. All the while, I remained stone silent, yet intensely aware that the pain heightened the pleasure for me. This man, too, became a regular. I would show up at the Rialto at about midnight and await the gent in the nice suit. Sometimes people would observe what he was doing to me, which made the experience even more exciting.

After my "gentleman" left, I would sit there shaking and trying to get a grip on myself. I was incapable of understanding any of this. It was all instinct and spontaneity. But thus began a new line of sexual exploration—seeking and finding sadist pedophiles in movie theaters. This was my secret world, and these were my secret pleasures. Had I thought about it at all, I might have said that my movie house adventures were my compensation for all the rage, pain, and misery I endured at home and in the Yeshiva.

It wasn't long before I began asking for rough sex. When a raincoat sat down next to me, I would loosen my belt and wrap it around my wrists. My suitor immediately got the message and took full advantage.

As I had learned before, my behavior was not at all uncommon. An entire S&M subculture existed in the movie theaters. One night, a man dressed as a cowboy sidled in next to me. After an initial round of foreplay, he pulled some rope out of his pocket and proceeded to tie up my genitals and then singe my arm with his cigarette lighter. People routinely showed up with handcuffs, cigarette lighters, and even knives.

Sometimes things got dangerous. One night, in a practically deserted theater, a man dressed in a military uniform tied me up and threatened to kill me. It terrified me beyond anything I had ever known. I was sure I wasn't getting out of the theater alive, but he became bored when I pretended to be drunk and stoned and incapable of responding to him. On another occasion, a teenage boy watched an older man masturbate me. When he was done, the teen sat next to me and demanded my money at knifepoint. I handed him my wallet, which contained a single dollar bill. Little did he know that I routinely kept my money in my sock. You learned what you needed to learn.

Yes, I was afraid from time to time. But when you are a young kid and desperate for physical pleasure, the dangers seem small and avoidable. Now, as I look back at that period of my life, I realize how utterly and completely alone I was, and how starved I was for any kind of physical contact.

Like everyone else, I learned what love was at home. And my experience of "love" was, in fact, manipulation and violence. Both were sugar-coated with the pretense of family and caring. Actually, no one in my family used the word love in connection with other family members. We "loved" chocolate and we "loved" our television set. But we never said that we loved each other, and certainly no one in our family was treated with any real love. My early experiences with sex were not much different. The sexual pleasures of arousal, touch, and orgasm were all very real, but they came from strangers and, in fact, as various forms of molestation. But just as

I was unfamiliar with love, I didn't know what to expect from sex. My parents had never spoken to me about either one. In the end, the sex I experienced was just about as abusive as the love had always been.

So I, Elliot Tiber, was driven to have sex with men, but that fact didn't really register with me at first. I took it for granted. It was not until much later, when I actually had sex with someone I liked, that my true nature announced itself.

❋   ❋   ❋

It was the summer I turned sixteen, just before I started college. One day, I decided to go to Riis Beach in Queens. Wearing my bathing trunks, I lay on a blanket and took in the sun. Eventually, someone put a blanket next to mine and lay down next to me. I noticed a handsome young man my own age, but I quickly turned away, and didn't let on. Soon, I felt a hand come up beneath my own and intertwine with my fingers. Surprised, I looked over at my neighbor and smiled. The young man smiled back at me and said his name was Barry.

"I'm Elliot," I said. "My friends call me Elli."

My first thought, as always, was: *How is it possible that such a handsome young man would have any interest in me?* But he clearly did. We talked for a couple of hours about movies and school. His hand kept caressing mine under the sand. All of this was new and exciting—a first love. Finally, I suggested he come back to my house. My parents and sisters were away and I knew I would have the house to myself. I had never had a boy come over to my house, and the excitement was almost unbearable.

As I unlocked the door to my home, I felt an immediate wave of shame rise within me. Our furniture was obtained from the Salvation Army; all the rejected stuff that the charity didn't want, we got for next to nothing. And it showed. The only room that had matching furniture was my sister Goldie's bedroom, which is where I led Barry immediately.

Barry was the first man I ever kissed. In fact, he was the first man with whom I experienced anything that might be called "making love." We kissed, had sex, and then actually talked about our lives. I told him that I was about to be an art student at Hunter College, but that I wanted to study at Brooklyn. He was about to go off to college in upstate New York. It seemed possible that we could become friends and actually see each other again. This alone was an entirely new experience for me—to have sex with someone whom I actually looked at and spoke to.

We spent the rest of the day and night talking and making love. All the while, Barry kept using the word "gay" in our conversation, especially in reference to himself. I had never used that word before. Even though I had been having sex exclusively with men, I had never labeled myself as a homosexual, partly because I had never connected to another human being during sex. Moreover, sex was something that I kept hidden, even from myself. It happened in darkened theaters with total strangers. And in most cases, I would not have wanted to be in any sort of relationship with those strangers, anyway.

Barry, on the other hand, did not think of himself as anything but a homosexual. He was comfortable with his sexuality. Moreover, Barry was seeking a relationship. He connected sex with relationships, and made me aware of that connection. He opened me up to my own need for a relationship, specifically with a homosexual man. All of this helped make me accept my next big revelation: *I'm gay.*

It couldn't have been more obvious, but until that moment, it had been an unknown fact of my humanity. Not only did I now realize something fundamental about myself—something that was always there—but it even had a name. Homosexual. Gay. It was as if a giant door that I didn't even know existed suddenly swung open and revealed an entirely new wing of my house, a wing that I may have vaguely suspected was there, but never really thought about before.

In fact, it didn't change very much. I was still me. But looking back, I realize that perhaps there was a new glow to life—a new pleasure that arose from knowing that I wasn't entirely alone.

The next morning, when we both woke up, Barry said, "Why don't I call my friend Harvey and ask him to come over? He's a playwright. You'll like him."

When Harvey arrived, Barry was in the shower, so I brought Harvey into the living room and we both sat on the sofa. We were just getting to know each other when Harvey reached over, put his arm around me, and kissed me full on the lips. He then leaned even closer to me and both of us embraced and engaged in an even more passionate kiss. This was the second person to kiss me in two days, and I was a bit in shock. Two handsome men found me attractive and wanted to kiss me. While on some level I didn't believe it, I could not deny my overwhelming pleasure in being desired.

Unfortunately, Barry chose that moment to come downstairs. Entering the living room, he caught us in full embrace. He threw a fit, got dressed, and stormed out of the house, never to be heard from again. I couldn't blame him. I tried to get in touch and explain, but he never returned my calls. Harvey and I saw each other for about a month before we, too, went our separate ways.

Once I was in college, my sexuality became more clear to me, even as I did my best to keep it hidden from others. In my freshman year, I joined a fraternity and pretended to be straight, like the other guys. At one of our parties, a redheaded woman—drunk and stoned—took a fancy to me and hauled me into one of the rooms where all the coats were piled on top of the bed. She proceeded to undress and insist that we make love. I accommodated her—in large measure to keep my cover—and it was a good thing, too. Suddenly, the door burst open and most of my fraternity brothers fell into the room, calling out my name as I had sex with this girl. We both moaned for the gallery, but I found the experience entirely repulsive.

When I was nineteen, a friend told me about a rough gay bar on Third Avenue where everyone wore leather jackets. "Do you want to go?" the friend asked.

"Sure," I said.

We showed up at the bar wearing cotton jackets, cotton pants, and regular street shoes. We stuck out like schoolboys in a whorehouse. Soon, a big biker-type guy, tall and muscular, spotted the two of us and walked directly over to me. He looked me up and down, gave me a mean expression, and then punched me hard in the shoulder. "Fuckin' fairy, you come here next Saturday and you better be wearing a leather jacket and boots." He didn't have to tell me twice.

I went to the local Army Navy store and bought a jacket and boots. When my friend learned that I had purchased the requisite clothing, he said, "You're not going back there, are you?"

"Of course I'm going back," I said.

"You're crazy," he said.

"Marlon Brando wears a leather jacket. Why can't I?"

The next Saturday, I showed up at the bar on Third Avenue looking as tough as everyone else. The same tall biker came up to me, looked me up and down, punched me again, and then kissed me. We spent the next three days at his apartment having thrilling S&M sex. And then, as with others both before and after, I never saw him again.

✻　　✻　　✻

After I graduated from college, I got an apartment in Greenwich Village and began working at W. & J. Sloane as an interior designer. I also did a lot of freelance design work for a steady stream of wealthy patrons. My career was rising fast and it wasn't long before I was mingling with the rich and famous of New York. Among my friends at the time was Alvin Epstein, a well-known Broadway and television actor. Alvin knew everybody in the arts and in Hollywood, it seemed, and he was constantly being invited to the best parties.

One night we met for drinks at the San Remo bar in Greenwich Village, a popular hangout for gays and the occasional celebrity. We had not yet finished our first drink when I recognized Marlon Brando and Wally Cox sitting at a nearby table. I elbowed Alvin and said, "Is that who I think it is?"

Alvin turned around and then smiled broadly. With that, he got up and walked over to the two men. Alvin, Brando, and Cox all burst into effusive greetings, followed by hugs. I trailed behind, but Brando and Cox insisted that the four of us sit together.

Brando oozed sexuality. It didn't matter if you were straight or gay; you couldn't look at the man without thinking of him in bed. Both Brando and Cox had been drinking for some time already, and both were already pretty loose.

Brando looked at me and said, "Hey, kid. What you staring at?"

Momentarily flustered, I said, "Is that really Mr. Peepers?" Wally Cox—who would later star in a number of very popular television shows, including *The Hollywood Squares*—had originally risen to fame as the title character of the 1950s sitcom *Mister Peepers*.

Cox turned to me and said, "No, I'm Orson Welles."

Brando laughed and said, "Nah, he's Rita Hayworth."

With that, I told Brando that people told me all the time that he and I could pass for twins.

Everyone broke into laughter and the fun began.

"Where are you from, guy?" Brando asked me.

"Me? I'm from Bensonhurst, Brooklyn, not far from Coney Island."

"Aren't you far from home?" he asked me. "Don't you know there are a lot of homos in this bar?"

"Shhh," I said. "People might hear you. In Bensonhurst, we don't have homos."

Everyone howled with laughter.

"Sure you do," Wally Cox said. "They're everywhere. Even in Coney Island. What would your parents say if they knew you were having a beer with homos? Barkeep, give our Brooklyn kid here another beer."

"I can't believe I'm having beer with Mr. Peepers and Stanley Kowalski," I said to Cox and Brando.

Brando replied. "Nah, I'm not him. I'm Eva Marie Saint."

"I'm saving up to buy a leather biker jacket," I said to Brando. And then in a low, conspiratorial whisper, I said to both of them, "Hey, are you both, uh, homosexuals?"

"No way," said Cox. "We came here to see some of them queers. But us? Not at all. Are you one of them?"

Brando cut in, "He's from Brooklyn, remember. They don't have them there." Everyone broke into laughter again.

"I don't know what to say," I said to both of them. "You're both here with ordinary people." And then gesturing to Brando, I said, "You won an Academy Award, for crying out loud."

Brando smiled and said. "Tell you what, kid. Give me a hug, but a manly hug."

"What about giving me a hug?" Cox said. "Don't you want to tell your Mom and Pop that Mr. Peepers and Marlon Brando bought you a beer and hugged you?"

I got up and, somewhat in awe, hugged them both.

"Tell you what," Brando said. "We're going to a party just a few blocks from here. Come to the party and we can hug all we want up there."

Wally Cox leaned toward me and, in a sly stage whisper, said, "But let me warn you. There might be quite a few homosexuals at the party."

That night I hung out with Marlon Brando, Wally Cox, Alvin Epstein, and a whole bunch of other celebrities, many of them homosexuals. And it was one of the best nights of my life.

Nights like this are rare in anyone's life. They are a great high, which for me was followed by a great low. But I was utterly alone when I got home that night. My few friends and relatives had someone to go home to—someone with whom they could share their great stories. That night, I lay alone in my bed. There was no one to hear about the night I spent laughing, hugging, and living it up with Marlon Brando and Wally Cox. I suppose I could have called one of my sisters, but they wouldn't have cared even if they did believe me, which was doubtful. And, of course, my parents wouldn't have any interest at all.

"Bran-who?" I could hear my mother saying. "Wally Cox? Who talks such nonsense? Listen, did you make any money today? The mortgage, it's killing us." And so, another long, slow, and painful fade-to-black night for Elli. Whenever the hard lonesomeness would engulf me, I would draw on my father's lifelong example— I'd simply go to sleep.

And that was my life. During the week, I worked in New York, where I made money and had occasional sexual liaisons with strangers. On Friday nights, I drove up to White Lake to save my parents' business.

In White Lake, I pretended to be a straight businessman. That, of course, was a gigantic lie. In New York, I was an artist and a gay man. That was the truth. But by pretending to be both, I couldn't be either—not fully, at least.

I was ripped apart by my two identities, unable to resolve the conflict I faced. If I chose my own life, I would flee White Lake like a man released from a Turkish prison, but then my parents would be destitute. Then again, if I didn't choose my own life, I might drive my car off the George Washington Bridge. Either way, the clock was ticking. Every Friday afternoon, as I drove north on the New York Thruway and my friends headed east for Fire Island, I ruminated darkly about the utter mess my life was in. My sister's prophetic warning often haunted me on those drives back to the motel. "You will throw away your good young years on that crappy motel," she said. "It will never work out."

So many times, I wanted to turn the car around and forget I ever knew those two dopes who took pleasure in destroying their lives and mine. There were times when I wanted to strangle them both. But I continued driving toward Exit 16, even as the tears ran down my face.

4

Digging a Deeper Grave While Laughing Hysterically

"You're going to do what?"

My therapist, Morris—an otherwise unflappable man—ripped the pipe from his mouth and, thanks to the sudden contraction of his gluteus maximus, performed a rather impressive vertical leap out of his leather chair. I wanted to give him a "9" for height, but in light of his flailing arms, could award only a "3" for style.

Morris was reacting to my latest scheme for attracting business to my motel.

"Install a swimming pool?" he asked in disbelief. "Are you out of your mind? You have to find a way to get the hell out of there! Each season, you bury yourself deeper and deeper in debt! I'm telling you, Elliot, you'll never earn a dime. You won't have any money when you're sixty-five, and you'll end up living in some public shelter with newspapers around your feet. Sell that place and get your life back!"

Sage advice, and at fifty bucks an hour, you'd think I'd listen. But I had succumbed to the same disease that plagues your average pathological gambler—which is to say, I kept thinking that if I took one more risk, I'd hit the jackpot.

The pool cost ten thousand dollars, which was a lot of money in 1968. However, I had painted an enormous mural of neo-Greco-Roman gardens at the Park Avenue penthouse of a baroness, who, I later learned, owned a car business under the Third Reich. The payment would cover the cost of the pool. The construction workers had already broken ground when the baroness's decorator, Paolo di Montipulciano, refused to pay me.

Paolo claimed my gardens weren't authentic, said he didn't like the artistic quality of the finished mural, and decided, once the painting was done, to put my paints on the street and lock me out of the apartment. I took the two deadbeats to court.

My case was a little stronger than either of them had assumed. Never one to brag, I hadn't told the Nazi baroness and her pock-marked Italian poodle that I was a teacher of fine arts at Hunter College. Nor did I mention that I had invited my department chair, Dr. Edna Leutz, to have a look at the painting one day when no one was in the penthouse. Dr. Leutz liked the work and decided to take some photographs, which I later showed to a couple of art historians. They verified the authenticity of the gardens in court. As far as the quality of the work, Dr. Leutz testified to that.

"Judge," I began, "I need this money for my mother, who walked from Minsk to New York in 1914, running from Cossacks who raped and defiled helpless Jewish families." In hindsight, I think I was telling this oft-repeated sob story partly to get some quiet revenge on my mother in public. "If my mother doesn't get this money," I continued, "I cannot pay for the pool that's being installed right now in our motel, which means we're sure to go bankrupt and my mother will be out on the street."

As fate would have it, the judge was the son of a Russian émigré himself, also from Minsk. Go figure.

"My mamma, may she rest in peace, probably was on that same refugee steamer with your mamma," the judge told me. "My mamma washed floors from Minsk to Minnesota in order to pay for my legal education." He then turned to Paolo the poodle and said, "Duke"—Paolo had claimed royal blood—"pay your bill or you're dead ravioli."

The pool was finally installed courtesy of the baroness, although without the cabana and assorted chaise lounges that I might have liked. In their place was a row of Salvation Army folding chairs. Beautiful as it was, the pool didn't attract any new business. The Teichberg Curse had once again sucked me in and spat me out—this time, with a big pool that would require constant upkeep.

☮   ☮   ☮

We started out in 1955 with a modest little guesthouse that had nine rooms. Two of those rooms were created when Momma hung curtains in the center of two large rooms—thus turning two rooms into four—and another by nailing a big box to the tree out back.

When things went as they were destined to go, which was straight downhill, we did the only logical thing we Teichbergs could think of—we built more buildings. By the early part of 1969, we were the proud owners of New York's ugliest and most dysfunctional motel and resort, complete with seventy-four rooms—a dozen of which were bungalows—and fifteen acres wedged between two intersecting highways, Route 17B and Route 55.

If you stood on Route 55, the northern border of our property, and looked south at the five main buildings of our motel, you might think that the place had been abandoned years ago. Our buildings were painted white, but vines had grown up along some of the walls. Here and there, patches of earth appeared between swaths of overgrown weeds. Behind one of the main motel buildings was our pool, which was surrounded by a motley collection of old chairs, none of which looked the least bit inviting. Just south of the pool and the main buildings sat our cluster of dilapidated bungalows, many of them teetering on uneven legs. The bungalows were located in the swamp, which, thanks to poor drainage and an ongoing sewage problem, rarely, if ever, dried up. There were days when you needed a good pair of galoshes to get to your bungalow's front door unscathed, but that was one of the many things we didn't like to talk about.

All of the expansion had been paid for by my New York artwork. I was able to do this, in part, because I entertained the fantasy that some day, some rich and beautiful man would drop out of the sky and put me on easy street for the rest of my life. Meanwhile, I maintained my other illusion—that we were running a legitimate motel.

To be perfectly frank, some of the rooms should not have been called "rooms." In a few of the larger spaces, I hung old shower curtains, many of them ripped and stained. I then placed artificial palm trees that I had obtained from my employer, W. & J. Sloane, against the curtains to reinforce the illusion of a wall. I had Pop hang exposed light bulbs from the ceiling, as we couldn't afford actual light fixtures. Sometimes, Pop had to improvise a little with the electricity, and more than once, he was forced to run the wiring over a shower fixture, a potentially lethal combination, but perfectly safe if the guest was careful. Anyway, thanks to the shower curtain and fake palm trees, we could turn an otherwise useless space into two rooms.

Of course, you couldn't hang numbers on such "rooms," but that was the least of my worries. Many of the doors didn't have doorknobs, and fewer still had keys. The mattresses were hard and lumpy; the linoleum, broken and blackened. The weeds often threatened to engulf parts of the property. And, of course, there were the empty air conditioner and television boxes, and the dummy phones that didn't work.

In the office, I hooked up some Christmas tree lights to the switchboard that the telephone repairman had sold us. The tiny lights went off randomly, and every so often the switchboard issued little buzzing noises that made it sound like it was working. When one of the guests came into the office and complained that his or her telephone wasn't functioning, I'd say that the repairmen were on strike. Consequently, service was delayed. My mother was quick to add that there were no refunds under any circumstances.

The office itself was a comic foray into trailer park kitsch. Originally, the place was no more than five by six feet in size, but Pop later expanded it so that we could serve coffee. The walls were plywood and bare, save for several signs that I had hung, such as "Motel for Sale—Make Me an Offer" or "Cash Only—No Refunds." The ceiling and floors were plywood, too. The latter was covered with cheap linoleum that was peeling and stained. Accenting this charming little setting was a pair of expensive red drapes that I had obtained from Sloane's. And hanging from the ceiling was the *pièce de résistance*—an elaborate crystal chandelier that could have held its own in the Ritz Carlton, but instead served as an ostentatious announcement to the world that we were the ridiculous Teichbergs, too far in the red to be embarrassed by our decorating choices.

Most people would have been too humiliated to be caught dead in such a motel. I had the job of convincing them to pay money to stay there. It wasn't easy. All of my creative skills were put to the test.

Among the bungalows that we purchased was a large cabin that the previous owners had used as a casino for bingo and card games. I put the thing on wheels and hauled it four hundred feet up the highway, finally placing it in front of our property. I got some chairs from a defunct bowling alley, rented a projector, and then hung a sign out front that announced our "Underground Cinema." The first film I showed was a melodrama about motorcyclists. I rented and showed other films, but the only customers were our local milkman, Max Yasgur, who quietly supported everything I did, and a few drunks who had just lost their shirts at the Monticello Raceway.

When I wasn't showing movies, I used the casino as an art gallery. No one showed up, except for Max and Elaine and Bill Grossinger, who owned and ran the biggest and most successful resort in the Catskills. I used to call Elaine for help. "Elaine, I'm dying over here. Send me some of your overflow, please."

"Elliot, I will tell people that if they need a place out of the rain, they should call you, but I'm going to explain that the place is a dump."

"Elaine, don't tell people we have radios, because we don't," I said to her. But feeling a little ashamed, I said, "We have TVs."

"Elliot, I know about your TV boxes."

Elaine was as good as her word, but soon stopped sending people because too many complained afterwards.

Complaints were part and parcel of doing business. Most of the people to whom we rented were little old Jewish ladies and gentlemen from New York whom I called *yentas*—Yiddish for those who gossip and talk endlessly about nothing. But every so often, we'd get someone of means who couldn't get a room at one of the better Catskill resorts, such as Grossinger's or The Concord. We never turned away any form of business, but we knew what to expect when such a person entered one of our rooms.

One day, a woman with a little dog under her arm came storming into our office and demanded her money back after seeing her room. "There's no air conditioning," she said, deeply offended. "I live at Sutton Place, and I wouldn't allow my servants to live under such vile conditions like these. I demand to see your membership number."

I sighed, looked at Momma, and let her field this one. She was all too eager.

"We don't rent to your kind of people," she said, her chest inflating like a proud peacock. "This is an exclusive motel. You want a number, pick a number, pick any number you want!" Momma began wagging her finger in righteous indignation, as if she were about to place a curse on the woman. "Only God will punish you for aggravating a mother who walked here from Russia. Go ahead then, Miss Bauble, pick a number and complain to the membership association." And with that, she pointed her finger to one of the signs that hung in our office: "No Refunds."

Once a motor club inspector arrived unannounced and took a room at our motel. Refined and gentlemanly, he was obviously used to reviewing properties that met high standards. As I recall, he was in his room for about twenty minutes before he returned to our office in a state of shock. "This dump is a disgrace to the hospitality industry," he said, as if on the brink of a coronary. "The proprietors should be imprisoned. Where are the owners?"

"Their main offices are located in the Berlin Hilton," I said.

The inspector continued, too upset to realize what I had just said. "The stained sheets don't look or smell as if they'd been laundered in twenty years."

"That's impossible," I said. "The motel has only been here eight years."

Again, my words didn't register. In utter disbelief, he said, "There are no towels. I had to tip a mad Russian maid two dollars in order to rent one. The TV is only an empty box. The phone is not connected to anything. The desk clerk has a barrel of keys without numbers. And I had to buy soap from that same maid. She even asked me to pay rent on the parking spot in front of my room. How dare you people put up a sign, 'Deluxe Accommodations'? I demand a full refund and an apology."

Suffice to say, Momma took over, and the inspector's demands were not met. Yet another dissatisfied customer.

In order to keep my sanity—not to mention the hope that I might escape this place one day—I hung signs all over the property, as well as along the highway leading to White Lake. We had five billboards and Pop and I built a few more. On one of the billboards, I wrote: "Roads Washed Away Ahead!!!! No U-Turns. Detour. Last Motel Before End of the Road!" Another read: "This Motel Not Affiliated with Hilton International, George V Paris, ITT Sheraton, Princess Grace."

On the property, I hung little signs on the motel walls, or posted them in the weeds. "Degenerates Welcome," "S&M Lovers

Club," and "Eagle' Nest." The Eagle's Nest was a gay club in Greenwich Village, but only gays knew that. The reference served as a form of code that did, in fact, flag down the occasional kindred spirit. The signs kept me busy—in more ways than one.

The signs were also necessary to me in the same way that a pressure cooker valve keeps the pot from exploding. I was a gay artist posing as a straight businessman, and that alone would make a sane person crazy. But throw such a person in with the likes of my parents and, well, you either painted signs or committed homicide, and I chose the signs.

I created a bar and had topless waiters—twenty-one-year-old boys wearing bikini underwear—serve the clientele, most of whom were women. In order to add a little excitement and fun, I placed a large board in the men's room with plenty of colorful magic markers so that the men could write all kinds of erotic graffiti. Then I told the women that if they bought a drink at midnight, they could go into the men's room and read what the men had written. I followed that idea by selling inexpensive white paper plates to the women for a dollar apiece. They could write whatever they wanted on the plates and then staple them to the walls and ceiling of the men's room. For a while, the women loved that, especially after they'd had a few drinks.

The bar was packed, but it was tiny—no bigger than twenty feet by thirty feet. By late evening, many of the men and women had found each other and were making out. That was the loneliest part of my job. And to make matters worse, the bar was too small to make any real money, and what money we did make found its way to Momma's brassiere. By the end of each month, we'd be broke and unable to pay the mortgage, which meant that I had to pour more money into the place to keep it alive.

On weekends, we needed to feed the few guests we had, so I ordered take-out at a nearby Chinese restaurant. I served the food on cheap paper plates purchased from a wholesale supplier that had gone bankrupt. In many cases, the plates still bore the names of the companies for which they were intended. When people were handed this "tablewear," they were aghast. "We can't eat food off these flimsy things," they said. So I hung a sign that read: "We're Not Responsible for Anything."

One of the yentas asked me, "Who's the crazy person who makes all these signs?"

"I don't know," I told her. "They just appear while we're asleep."

In order to attract more business, I opened Yenta's Pancake House, where Pop and I cooked breakfast. We had a limited menu, to say the least, but even the few meals we offered were challenging to Pop. Someone would say, "I want my English muffin well done." And Pop, whose roofer hands were permanently stained with tar, would look at the guest as if she were from outer space. "The way it comes out is the way you'll eat it," he snapped.

I was constantly searching for ways to balance the limitless charm of my parents, so I hung more signs: "Barbra Streisand pancakes—$40.00." "Ethel Merman pancakes—$60.00." And then, next to the Ethel Merman sign, I wrote, "Today only—$45.00."

Out of desperation for a little social life, I created a swingin' singles night. I ran ads in *The Village Voice* saying, "Fed up with Fire Island? Would you believe White Lake—at half the price? Swingin' Singles Weekends," after which I gave directions to our motel. I got lots of losers, drunks, and misfits—even a bald-headed clergyman who kept asking me if I believed in God. When I asked him if *he* believed in God, he quietly said "Once," and left the motel without another word.

The list of jobs I did around the motel seemed endless. During any given day, I served as toilet bowl cleaner, room renter, lawn mower, cook, pool boy, cesspool cleaner, guest relations manager, hotel security, fat son, and general schlepper. Life became a continuous cycle of cleaning toilets and making pancakes. Most days, there wasn't enough time to get to it all.

When I had a minute to rest, I often retreated to bungalow number two, which was my personal hideaway. There was an old, lumpy cot and some of my leather and S&M gear hanging from the ceiling. The place looked like a dungeon that was well-equipped with all the latest torture devices. I would sprawl on the cot, exhausted, under a hanging mobile of whips and handcuffs. I was so depressed that a career as a rabbi in Flatbush started to look like a missed opportunity. When I finally relaxed and let my mind wander, I often fantasized about some rich, gorgeous stranger showing up and sweeping me off to Paris. And then my mother's voice would come bellowing over the grounds and pierce my reverie through the heart. "Elli!" she screamed. "The toilet bowls need cleaning. Oy, what what a mess, and my back is killing me!"

I had other diversions, however. One of them, whom I'll call Bill Smith, was married and a co-owner of one of the largest and most exclusive hotels in the Catskills. He was gay and needed an outlet. I was the outlet. He'd come over to my place and we'd spend an hour or two in my dungeon bungalow. Every so often, he'd call to make a date. He thought he was being discreet but, unbeknownst to both of us, Maria, the town operator, would listen in on our phone conversations. Maria was married to Rusty, an adorable little construction worker. The two of them lived across the street from us and were bored silly with each other. Maria listened in on phone conversations for recreation. We gave her an earful.

One day, Maria admitted to me that she knew why Bill Smith's car was regularly seen parked in front of our motel.

"Maria," I said, with mock disapproval. "That's not nice. In fact, it's illegal."

"I know," she said, suddenly pouting. "But you have the only interesting conversations in the whole town."

Just a few years after I started running our motel, I decided to join the Bethel Chamber of Commerce. I quickly discovered that it was as dysfunctional as the Teichberg motel. Meetings were more gab sessions among the yentas than any serious attempt to create business for our community. Even more dispiriting, I was the best-educated member of the Chamber, and the only one with any ideas for improving our desperate fortunes. The other Chamber members already knew me well and were aware of my reputation for zany attempts at creating businesses. None of my endeavors ever worked, but in a town that had surrendered to failure long ago, I looked like the only living member of the Chamber. Thus, by unanimous vote, I was elected president of the Bethel Chamber of Commerce. *E Pluribus Unum.*

The members were thrilled. And now came the really exciting moment—they wanted to tell me their big idea to bring tourist dollars to Bethel. The former president, a sixty-something named Ethel, clasped her hands together and announced with unbridled excitement, "Elliot, we want to build a monorail!" The six or so ladies and two men looked at me with wide-eyed anticipation. "What do you think, Elliot? Isn't it a great idea?"

Another enthusiastic voice quickly chimed in. "Disneyland has a monorail, Elliot. And it brings in lots of business. We want to build a monorail that goes from New York City directly to Bethel. We could even have all the windows painted black. That way, passengers won't be able to see anything between New York and our little town. We think people will come from all over the country to ride our monorail."

My mind and I were having a little meeting of our own while this was going on. Here is the transcript: *What is it about Bethel that attracts the lunatics? Maybe we're on some weird grid line— the land-based equivalent of the Bermuda Triangle—where mysterious powers converge to make everyone demented. Or maybe aliens are conducting experiments on us at night while we're asleep and the side effects include psychosis. Or maybe it's the water. Yep, it's definitely the water.*

"Who's going to underwrite such a project?" I asked, trying hard not to let on that I thought they were nuts.

"We don't know, Elliot, but we know that you can do anything," one of them said.

"Okay," I said, "we'll put it on the agenda, but let's try to do something smaller before we tackle a multimillion-dollar project. What other ideas do you have?"

They looked around at each other, suddenly at a loss. Finally, Ethel spoke. "Well, that's it, Elliot," she said. "We got so excited about the monorail that everything else seemed kind of boring by comparison."

"Nothing else came to mind?" I asked in disbelief.

Louie, a local plumber, had an idea. "Well, we did talk about putting up an information booth on your property—seeing how it stands at the entrance to White Lake and all." Suddenly embarrassed, he quickly added, "Ahh, we weren't going to do it without your permission, Elliot. But we could put brochures in the booth for all the businesses and touristy things people can do here. We thought that might attract visitors."

"Great idea, Louie," I said, suddenly relieved and grateful for the ray of sanity. "I'll even donate the lumber to build the thing." And that's what we did. Pop built a tourist information booth on our property, right on Route 17B, which was one of the main entrances to White Lake. Soon, it became a gathering place for the little old ladies who sat in their folding chairs and told tourists which attractions to see, and where to stay.

Unfortunately, Leon La Peters, who owned the largest bungalow colony in White Lake, and thus was the town's biggest taxpayer, got wind of the yentas' guidance. One day, La Peters, whom we called La Penis, drove his tractor across the road and flattened the booth. My first thought when I saw the deed was, *I hope no one's in there.* La Penis didn't care. He saw himself as General Patton in one of his tanks. The booth was the enemy and once it was down, he made sure it wasn't getting up again. He backed his tractor up and made several round trips over the flimsy pine boards until they were nothing but toothpicks. As he drove away, he raised his fist and growled, "I don't need no booth telling people where to stay in White Lake."

It wasn't long after that that La Peters had a fire—all his bungalows mysteriously burned to the ground. He collected on his insurance, moved to Miami, and set up a new bungalow colony that was even bigger than his first one.

When I heard the news, I ran into the office and said to my mother, "Where's Pop?"

"Down at the swamp, washing the sheets," she told me.

I ran down there, stepping carefully to avoid ruining my shoes, and said, "Pop, we're going to have a fire."

As he hosed down the sheets, Pop looked at me, slightly confused.

"We don't have any insurance," he said.

"I know," I said. "We'll get insurance."

"How can we have a fire, we're so spread out," he said.

I looked back at our property and realized he had a point. Sure, one building could go up in flames, but it was unlikely that the others would—at least not without a gasoline trail.

"Yeah, you're right," I said, more than a little deflated. "A fire's no good. Damn! Well, it didn't feel right anyway." I started to walk away, but then turned and looked back at my father, who was still giving his attention to the sheets.

"So, Pop, you've thought this through already, have you?" I asked him.

He didn't say anything. He just kept watering the sheets.

& egrave;ù   èù   èù

One good thing did come of my role as President of the Chamber of Commerce, however. I had the legal authority to issue myself an official town permit to conduct my annual music and arts festival. There were no zoning laws to speak of in White Lake. I simply typed up a permit, giving myself legal permission to hold a rock concert—such as it was. My father built a stage, twenty by twenty feet, and I hung a couple of big spotlights above it. They weren't real spotlights, just big lights that I attached to a few tall poles overlooking the stage.

Every year, I had anywhere from six to a dozen local bands perform. Most of them were kids who barely knew how to play their instruments. But they got a big kick out of playing, even though the audience was limited to a handful of tourists, Max Yasgur, and several local drunks, most of whom were probably deaf—if not before the concert, then certainly afterwards. Once the bands concluded, I got out my own records and played LPs by the best new rock groups like The Byrds, The Animals, The Mamas & the Papas, and later artists like The Doors, Joe Cocker, Janis Joplin, The Jimi Hendrix Experience, and Cream. Occasionally, I would even play my Barbra Streisand albums to win some added yenta attendance. I did this every year for about eight years—for most of the '60s. In fact, people got so used to my putting on these concerts that they took the annual event for granted.

✹ ✹ ✹

In the late 1960s, my father's health began to fail. He had long endured the pain and discomfort of colitis, and unbeknownst to us, he now began to suffer the early stages of colon cancer. We had a barn on our property where he kept his roofing supplies, but it soon became apparent that he could no longer be a roofer. So I put an ad in *The Village Voice* and other New York newspapers, inviting a theater troupe to come to White Lake. "Freeland Summer Theater—sweat equity. I have the barn, you build the theater." Pretty soon, we had a whole gaggle of actors trooping into White Lake. Not long after, that "troop" became a troupe and the barn became a real live theater, complete with stage, bleacher seats, lighting, and curtain. I provided free rent and all the pancakes they could eat. Max Yasgur showed up with free yogurt, cheese, and eggs.

We went through a few summers of theater troupes, but in the spring of 1969, we landed a wonderful group of actors known as the Earthlight Players. Made up of thirty hungry artists and musicians, the group was very much in the spirit of the times. We gave the actors our original guesthouse, which they turned into a little commune. They made improvements in the theater and even chopped down a few trees to make new supports for the bleacher seats. We had no money to pay them, so they picked up odd jobs around town, and got by on pennies. Meanwhile, they rehearsed their summer play schedule, which I loved, but realized would go unattended by the locals.

"Nobody is going to come to see Chekhov's *Three Sisters*," I told them, "unless you do it in the nude. *Waiting for Godot?* Forget about it. These people are already living in that play and don't know it."

But the Earthlight Players didn't believe me. Besides, they were actors and committed to their craft. And like most theater people, they insisted that magic was going to happen.

On the other hand, I knew that we had better get some business soon. In May of 1969, cash flow was so bad, and we were so deep in the red, that we could not pay the mortgage on the place. I was desperate for money, so I called my sister, Goldie, who had married a multimillionaire. "Just give me a loan for five thousand dollars until the end of the summer," I pleaded. "It's tourist season. Fourth of July is coming. We're bound to have business. I'll be able to pay you back no later than September."

"Let them sink, Elli," she told me. "What are you doing? You're wasting your life. Let the government take the place already."

"The bank is going to repossess by the end of the season if I can't come up with the money to pay the mortgage," I told her.

"Good. Let them take it. They'd be doing you a favor."

So I went to the bank manager and pleaded for time. "Business is bad at the moment," I told him. "But things will pick up during the summer. Give me until the end of the season and we'll be able to pay the mortgage." Okay, he said. He'd carry us until the end of the summer, but no longer.

Pop and I painted the place and made it look as spiffy as we could—which, given the true condition of the motel, was not too spiffy. Weekends were a hell of intense physical labor and nonstop anxiety. My only reprieve came on Sunday nights when I got back in the Buick and raced to Greenwich Village. Once there, I went straight to one of the S&M clubs, hoping that a good whipping would exorcise some of my demons.

5

Stonewall
and the
Seeds of Liberation

The bar was sprawling and dark, with a great music system and plenty of room to dance. About two hundred people filled the room, most of them gay men, with a dozen or so lesbians thrown into the mix. People were dancing under the psychedelic lights, hunting for partners, or connecting with a potential lover, at least for the night.

Every so often, a bunch of us would break into song, especially when one of Judy Garland's records was being played. Judy had died the week before at a rented home in London. And on this day, just hours before we gathered at this bar, she had been laid to rest. For gay men, Judy's death was akin to having a family member pass away—the good family member who loved and understood you, the one you never had but wished you did. Judy embodied that tragic me-against-the-world spirit that every homosexual knows all too well. Her through-the-roof screaming, tormented joy, and drug-laced pathos reached us as few singers could. She sang our pain. Her bravery showed us how to cope with life. And now she was gone. And everybody at the Stonewall Inn, a hole in the wall on Christopher Street in the Village, was feeling angry and heavy of heart.

It was Friday night in late June. I usually went back to White Lake on Friday nights, but I had decided to stay in New York for a night of debauchery and maybe some revelry, too. Judy would have wanted us to sing and celebrate. I had nothing else on my mind but to drink myself silly, have a good time, and maybe find someone in one of Stonewall's darkened corners.

The previous Sunday, I had fled White Lake like a man running from the ghost of Hanukkah past. I was running from myself, of course, or more accurately, from the gathering storm of creditors and karma that was about to consume my motel, my parents' future, ten years of my life, a decade's worth of my income, and the pathetic fairy tale that I could save my parents from their own sui-cidal incompetence. What had I been thinking? Goldie was right! They were committed to destroying themselves and anyone who got mixed up with them. Oh, yes, the ghost of Hanukkah past—an old rabbi, no doubt, complete with black suit and hat, long beard, and payess—was about to step out from behind the bank, lift his great foot high in the air, and crush me, perhaps while I was still in the Buick. "You should have been a rabbi, Eliyahu!" I could hear him saying, just before he turned me into a potato pancake. "You think you went to Yeshiva so you could paint silly signs and rent motel rooms with no TVs?" I could almost see my Yeshiva rabbis nodding their heads in agreement.

Of course, these were just my petty crimes, the ones that surfaced when I wasn't going to the heart of things. Deep down, I knew the real reason that everything was going to hell in my life. I was cursed for being gay.

It wasn't until I saw the great skyline of Manhattan that the sweat on my brow began to dry. Somehow, the emerald city, with its unconditional acceptance and long parade of phalluses, allowed me to better accept myself. Even my breathing changed when I saw the Empire State Building, the greatest dick of 'em all. Finally, I was home again.

In White Lake, I was a loser, a *schlemiel,* an uneasy and closeted gay man whose cover was always in danger of being blown. But in Manhattan, I was a successful interior designer, a leading member of the NSID (National Society for Interior Designers), and a teacher at Hunter College. I was also part of the avant-garde community of designers, painters, photographers, actors, and writers who shaped the tastes for all of America. Although the average man or woman on the streets of Houston, Phoenix, or Peoria may not realize it, virtually everything people regard as fashionable or trend-setting is either influenced or directly produced by gay designers and artists, most of them living in New York or San Francisco. Even the trends that have been set by megastars such as Madonna, or the punk rockers, or the kids wearing "goth" make-up and clothes, all share the same source: the creativity of gay men, many of whom first revealed these new fashion statements in the S&M clubs of major cities.

The vital energies of our lives flow into every artistic and creative endeavor. Name any artistic field—novels, plays, poetry, painting, acting, design—and you will find gay artists among those making revolutionary contributions. In fact, this is true of virtually every important field, including business and the sciences. The irony is that historically, even though Americans have loved the contributions of gay people, they have hated the artists and inventors themselves.

History is the story of majorities oppressing minorities of one kind or another. In America, at mid-twentieth century, the two worst fates you could have were being gay and being black, and some have argued that being gay was the greater offense.

✳   ✳   ✳

In the 1950s and '60s, homosexuality was regarded by medical experts as a form of mental illness. Psychiatrists treated it as a disease that could be "cured" with Freudian analysis, hypnotherapy, or, if all else failed, electroshock "treatments." Psychoanalysts wanted us to believe that it was an aberration of our upbringing, a psychological disorder resulting from distorted relationships with mother and father. I fit the bill perfectly—but so did all of my straight friends. In fact, I didn't know a single gay or straight human being who didn't have a screwed-up childhood. Nevertheless, being gay was a disorder that therapists assured us could be "straightened out" with the right kinds of behavioral modifications. They couldn't cure anything else, but this they could cure.

There was also a belief that homosexuality was a choice that we could control—if we wanted to. Many so-called therapists and clergy thought that some people chose to be gay because they were evil. Hence, the attraction to an evil lifestyle. This belief gave license to all kinds of hate crimes against human beings whose only offense was a sexual orientation over which they had no control.

The truth is that nearly every young boy who discovers he is homosexual faces a life crisis that includes thoughts of suicide.

Rejected by family members, friends, and society at large, he is utterly alone and hated. All too many decide that suicide is the only way out. For those who choose to stay alive, many try to go straight. Some eventually marry and have children, others become priests, and still others try to live asexually. Virtually all of these attempts at "rehabilitation" and "redemption" fail. Try as they might, people cannot deny their sexual nature. Indeed, denial often leads to aberrant behaviors and even greater pain, not just for them, but for others, too.

Eventually, we learn that our only real redemption can be found in being ourselves. But we do that at a high price. "Coming out" meant that you are suddenly visible—or at least more visible. As a result, you are an easier target, not just for the thugs and homophobes, but for the law.

Homosexual behavior was illegal in the 1950s and '60s. In New York, cops used to set traps for gay men in Central Park and other locations around the city. Sporting tee-shirts, chinos, and colorful handkerchiefs hanging from a single back pocket—the handkerchiefs were code among gays for top or bottom—cops would pose as gay men. "Hey, what are you doing tonight?" an incognito cop would ask a man he thought might be gay. When the man answered and approached the cop, he got handcuffs slapped on his wrists and was thrown in the paddy wagon for a trip downtown. A lot of gay men arrived at the station bloodied and bruised, perhaps with a few ribs broken, thanks to the "justice" meted out on the way to the police station.

If you ran a gay bar or restaurant, you were subjected to routine raids. According to the police, there were laws on the books that prohibited people of the same sex from dancing together. Once the cops burst in, they demanded IDs and confiscated many of them. They then beat up drag queens or those who were deemed too effeminate, and threw them in jail for a night or two—where they were subjected to further abuse by other prisoners.

Many employers harbored similar attitudes. Unless you worked for a homosexual, your job was in jeopardy the moment your boss suspected that you were gay. In the 1950s and '60s, there were no laws against sexual discrimination. Men were fired on a moment's notice for the mere suspicion of homosexuality.

The attitudes of the police, the courts, and employers gave tacit permission to thugs and gangs who chose to express their homophobia in the most violent way possible. Beatings were commonplace and taken for granted—they were hardly considered a crime. What was far scarier was that homosexual men were routinely killed for no other reason than being gay.

Every gay man has his own stories of violence, and I am no different.

Once, I was coming out of Lenny's Hideaway—a gay bar in Greenwich Village—with a friend, and soon realized that we were being followed by a teen thug. My friend and I both got scared and started to walk faster. We didn't run, though, because we didn't want to let him know that we were running scared, which is exactly what we were doing.

"Where you fags running to?" the thug asked, quickly moving in front of us.

"Where you fags running to?" he repeated, this time with real malice in his face. We said nothing.

"That's a real nice watch you're wearing, faggot," he said to me. "I think you're going to give me that watch."

Like cowardly lightning, the young man I was walking with bolted, leaving me behind. The thug and I watched him tear off.

Never a fast runner, I feared that if I followed suit, I would be easily caught and matters would go far worse for me.

"Here, take the watch and leave me alone, okay?" I said.

"Gimme your wallet, fag, or I'll slice you up," he said. And with that, he produced a knife from his pocket.

I threw my wallet in his face and ran as fast as I could. I didn't look back until I was several blocks away, in a well-lit part of the city where I could duck into a store if I had to.

This was standard operating procedure: Gay men did not fight back. That was the unwritten rule. We turned the other cheek—for practical reasons. For one thing, we tended to be nonviolent. For another, if we were ever caught in a fight or if we happened to hurt or kill our assailant, no court in the country would view our actions as a matter of self-defense.

It was one thing to be attacked when you were with someone, but quite another when you were alone. One night, at the Amsterdam Theater on Forty-Second Street, a young man sat down behind me, rested his foot on the back of my chair, and pressed it into my shoulder and neck. I turned around and looked into a pair of dark, cruel eyes that showed clear intent to harm. I got up and left the theater, hurried down the street, and ran into an all-night diner. Once there, I took a seat in a booth and tried to catch my breath.

"Coffee, please," I told the waitress who suddenly appeared at my elbow. I was clearly shaken.

The place was nearly empty and I could see a row of empty booths before me. Suddenly, a high-pitched bell rang at the doorway to the diner and a long, dark raincoat brushed past my arm. The raincoat sat in the booth directly in front of me. This time, though, I could see the man clearly. He was quite dark, even swarthy, and in his early thirties, with oily black hair, dark stubble, and malevolent eyes that looked directly into mine. He sneered at me. Then he grabbed a silver chain that hung around his neck, played with it a bit, and jerked it tight, as if he were strangling himself. Something in those eyes told me that this was what he had in mind for me.

His eyes caught the silver bracelet that I wore on my right wrist.

"I like that ID bracelet, you fuckface piece of shit," he said. "Give it to me or I'm going to scar you up so nobody's ever going to want you."

I was shaking badly. I got up from the booth and left the diner quickly, but the young man was right behind me. Then, in a flash, he was in front of me.

"Where you goin', bitch?" he asked me. "You live around here?"

"No," I said. "I don't want any trouble, okay?"

"I've seen you in that theater a lot," he said, "punching your package. That ain't nothin' compared to what I'm gonna do to you."

With that, he pulled out a police ID and badge and shoved it in my face. Then he pushed me hard into an alley that ran along the side of the diner. Once he had me against the wall, he reached down, grabbed my testicles, and started to squeeze.

Terrified beyond measure, I summoned all my strength and punched him directly in the eye. He reeled backward, grabbing his eye, and fell to his knees.

I ran faster than I had ever run in my life. I didn't stop running until I reached a bus that had just begun boarding passengers. I jumped onto the bus, found some change in my pocket—my God, for once I had exact change!—and let the slow behemoth roll out of danger.

More often than not, the cops were the enemy. Even when they weren't attacking us, they weren't protecting us either. If a gay man was beaten up in a public toilet and then went to the cops, the cop would laugh. "You got what you deserve, fairy," they'd tell us. Rights that most Americans took for granted became shaky the minute a cop suspected that you were gay.

Of course, gays congregated in places where they could feel comfortable and safe. We had Fire Island; Riis Beach Number 1; and Provincetown, Cape Cod, but even in these places, there could be trouble.

How can you escape feelings of self-hatred when you are so vehemently despised by society? Internalized homophobia plagued a great many of us. It was the first big disease that afflicted our community, and it paved the way for HIV and AIDS.

When you don't expect to be loved, sex becomes a purely physical experience. Its pleasures, its physical and emotional highs, and its pure energetic release provide escape from the prison of loneliness and outright rejection by the straight world. The sheer experience of being desired, if only sexually, becomes a validation of your life. Being desired becomes a reason to go on living. Sexual touch, however one defines it, becomes an antidote to the existential isolation that settles into the bones and blood of so many gay men.

When society hates you for your sexual behavior, sex becomes a revolutionary act and for many, an act of anger. It is a raised middle finger, a thumb in the eye to all those who despise you. It confirms difference. It insists on the right to life. It is a series of explicit, in-your-face photographs by Robert Mapplethorpe. It is the unstoppable power that comes with the ownership of every passing breath.

Given all the conflicting emotions surrounding sex, promiscuity was not only predictable for gays, but a virtual guarantee. It felt like our only right. For many of us, myself included, promiscuous sex became a way of life. It wasn't until the late 1960s that bathhouses became popular. But prior to the bathhouses, being gay—for most of us—meant cruising bars, sex clubs, and other places where we could meet gay men, mostly for anonymous sex.

All of this happened in secret, or at least hidden from the larger straight society. We were a community apart, an underground that unfortunately was festering with anger, feelings of profound injustice, and an acquired and perpetual disavowal of self. Of course, these conditions eventually contributed to a deadly epidemic. But what else could you expect?

Internalized homophobia infected most of the gay men and lesbian women I knew. It didn't matter how rich or talented you were—you never escaped the condemnation at the core of your being. You were gay, which meant that you were unworthy of acceptance and love—especially your own.

* * *

One night, I dropped in on a party at a large apartment on the Upper East Side. As I entered the living room, I saw a dense circle of men, all directing their attention toward something in the center of the room. The men were laughing, making wild gestures, and cheering whatever was taking place within the circle.

When I had finally worked my way through the crowd, I saw actor Rock Hudson sprawled out on the floor, naked and unconscious. Wow, Rock Hudson—Hollywood royalty. And here he was, lying on a hardwood floor, receiving pillow talk of an especially ugly kind. His beautiful features were distorted by drink and drugs.

He was the picture of vulnerability. His mouth was open and slightly ajar, his hair wet and pulled to one side. He lay on his back, fully exposed and available for groping and other sexual acts. A group of five or six guys were lined up and took turns getting on top of the handsome actor and having their way with him. All of this was taking place to cheers and catcalls. Hudson had been reduced to a slab of flesh, something people could use and brag about at dinner parties when their egos needed a boost. I couldn't look at what was happening for very long, and soon turned away. It wasn't the sex that bothered me—it was the rank dehumanization of someone who thought that, for once, he could safely be himself.

Excess was the theme of the times. But it was also an essential way to get through life, especially if you were homosexual. Better living through chemistry, we used to say. Drugs and booze made the hiding and the lying about one's identity easier to bear. In that way, none of us was any different from Rock Hudson, who was the archetypal gay man of the 1950s, '60s, and '70s. Hudson lived out the gay lie on a grand scale, beloved actor and ladies' man by day, closeted homosexual and terrified human being by night. And like the rest of us, he needed all the drugs and booze he could get his hands on to escape the irreconcilable identities that were at war within him. Eventually, he died of the gay disease—which I have referred to as self-rejection, but others call AIDS.

I imagined that gay men had something in common with black men; we both believed, correctly, that a great many of our problems stemmed from society's fear and hatred of us. That's how I interpreted many of my own troubles—at least those that I didn't pin on my insane parents and tortured childhood. Certainly, that's how I came to understand the self-destructive spiral that was killing two of the greatest artists I ever met—Tennessee Williams and Truman Capote.

When I moved to midtown Manhattan, I soon discovered that I was living in the same building as Tennessee, famed American playwright and author of such classics as *A Streetcar Named Desire, The Glass Menagerie,* and *Cat on a Hot Tin Roof.* In time, I got to know him, and the two of us spent many hours commiserating by the pool in our building. Tennessee was a heavy drinker and addicted to pills, especially after he lost his longtime lover, Frank Merlo, who died in the early '60s. But even when he was under the influence, Tennessee was a great raconteur and I used to love to listen to him speak. One day, on Third Avenue, I bumped into him as he was walking with Truman Capote. I was a big admirer of Capote's—I absolutely loved his writing, as well as his unique personality. Capote had already written *In Cold Blood* and was an international celebrity. And he was instantly engaging—enormously witty and provocative.

After Tennessee introduced us, Truman said, "I have always been partial to tall, good-looking young men. Are you married?"

"No," I told him smiling.

"Oh my God, I don't get to meet many virgins," he said, giggling. He giggled a lot, I soon found. Truman was Tweety Bird on coke. He was that rare combination of dirty old man and cherubic angel in a young boy's body. I was instantly smitten.

Tennessee suggested that we duck into a nearby bar and talk awhile. We drank and discussed plays, books, and my status as a virgin. I was thrilled to be boozing with two literary giants. I did not let on that I was a fat, ugly Yeshiva graduate from Bensonhurst. In fact, the subject never came up.

A few weeks later, Tennessee and Truman knocked on the door to my apartment. When I let them in, I realized instantly that the two were high on something—on everything, probably. They were

both giddy and barely conscious. Tennessee gave me a pill to take—
"Here, take one of these, and don't call me in the morning," he
slurred. Pretty soon, none of us was feeling any pain. I had told
them both of my proclivity for leather and S&M, and Truman
wanted to see me in my cop outfit. "I want to see the handcuffs,"
he kept saying in that childlike, inimitably high-pitched whine of
his. "Show me the handcuffs!"

I dressed in my police getup and modeled it for them.

"You're drooling, Tru," Tennessee said. "Maybe if you sucked
off a cop today, you wouldn't be so depressed." With that, he
pushed Truman toward me.

Truman fell at my knees, unzipped my pants, and did as
instructed. He then promptly collapsed on the floor and passed
out. It wasn't long before all three of us were asleep on the floor.
When we woke up, we all had Pepsis, which they used to chase
down yet another round of pills. I begged off, knowing it was time
to stop, but Tennesse and Truman fled their respective depressions
through a constant flow of drugs.

A few weeks later, I saw Tennessee by the pool and sat down
next to him. He looked depressed and I asked him what was wrong.

"I'm working on a play that isn't going well. I hate it. I'm sure
the critics will be devastating. I've been writing it over and over
again. Want a drink?" He handed me a thermos filled with coffee
and brandy.

"Is Tru okay?" I asked. "He could hardly walk out of my apartment that night."

"What are you talking about?" Tennessee asked. "Why was Tru
in your apartment?" In the course of further conversation, it
dawned on me that he didn't recall anything that had happened
just a few weeks before. I never saw Truman Capote again, and

soon thereafter, Tennessee moved. Years later, I saw him again at Chicago's Goodman Theater, where his second-to-last play, *A House Not Meant to Stand,* was being performed. He seemed stoned, alone, and depressed. He looked like a large piece of fruit that was collapsing in on itself. I didn't think he'd last long after that, and he didn't.

At the time, I didn't know many of the details of the two writers' lives—details that are widely known today, thanks to numerous biographies and films. As far as I was concerned, though, Tennessee and Truman suffered from many of the same ills that were tearing my own life apart. Being gay meant that in a deep region of your being, in some fundamental place that you recognize as your most vulnerable and true self, you are inherently guilty of being a criminal.

At this period in history, most gay men, no matter how gifted, led tragic lives. And while there may have been many reasons unrelated to being gay, most could not find healing or redemption in lasting love. The alternative—promiscuity, self-hatred, alcohol, and drugs—while offering short-term escape, usually led to destruction, just as they as they did with Tennessee Williams and Truman Capote.

Not everyone was promiscuous or angry, however. Many gay and lesbian people did, in fact, maintain long-term, loving, and committed relationships. Many were able to overcome homophobia and find love—love of self and love of another. But even these relationships, beautiful as they often were, had to be kept secret. And when one of the partners became sick or died, the surviving lover had no legal rights and no insurance benefits. No love could be considered pure if it was between two homosexual people.

We were hated because we were sexually attracted to someone of the same sex. Our lives were seen as worthless, even threatening. And far too many of us—myself included—accepted the verdict that we were somehow subhuman, and therefore unworthy of full citizenship on earth.

That is, until that Friday night in June 1969.

☮   ☮   ☮

At first, it was just another night of partying at the Stonewall. People were having a good time until about one-twenty in the morning, when the bartender jumped up on the bar and shouted, "Hey, the cops are coming! Quick, everyone, grab a girl to dance with. No same-sex dancing, no same-sex dancing!" With that, the bartenders grabbed their cash boxes and ran out of the bar through a back door.

I remember first hearing a beer bottle shatter against the floor somewhere in the room. Then, from inside the slowly growing bedlam, someone shouted, "Don't let the pigs harass us anymore! Don't let them in this bar! Fuck it, man, tonight we're fighting back!"

I was shocked. This had never happened before. We were used to the raids—we knew the drill, and it never included fighting back. Now, suddenly, there was the smell of revolution in the air. The room was full of fever and fury, and my anger ignited. I ran over to the front doors with two others and we threw the heavy metal bars that locked the doors from inside. Then a bunch of us pushed the jukebox in front of the doors, blocking the entrance. Immediately, others joined in, pushing tables and chairs against the doors, as well. Now the cops were outside, their squad car lights flashing and bullhorns sounding. They pounded on the doors and threatened to arrest us all if we didn't open up.

Someone screamed, "There's more of us than them! Let's beat the shit out of 'em!" It registered again that this was the first time I had ever heard anything like that. We were finally taking on the cops.

Anger welled up inside me—a terrifying anger that had festered and grown over the years. Unbelievably, I heard myself yell, "Let's go out there and turn over their fucking cars!"

Suddenly, everyone was screaming at the top of their lungs. We cleared the barricades from the front doors and streamed out onto Christopher Street. Only then did we realize that there were only a couple of police cars and perhaps four or five cops waiting for us.

Once we were outside, a group of us joined hands and started yelling, "Gay power! Gay power!" At first, there was no violence, but then one of the cops grabbed a butch lesbian and dragged her toward a cop car. Courageously, she resisted arrest and started yelling, "Gay power! Gay power!" And then all hell broke loose.

People started screaming at the cops. We broke ranks and a bunch of us gathered around one of the cop cars, rocked it back and forth, and heaved it onto its side. The thrill of tossing a cop car gave me a feeling of power I had never experienced before. Those around me felt the same. We were wide-eyed with power and ready to fight. The cops were frantic. They were calling for support, and soon more cops arrived in paddy wagons and squad cars, lights flashing and sirens screaming.

The mob got chairs from inside the Stonewall and started flinging them at the cops. Others were throwing bottles, rocks, and sticks that they had found in Sheridan Park, across from the Stonewall, and still others were throwing pennies. Cops were beating people with their nightsticks, or throwing them into squad cars and paddy wagons.

As if out of nowhere, a few hundred more people showed up in Sheridan Park—gay men and lesbians, all ready to take on the cops. Several of us jumped on top of car hoods and roofs and started chanting for the mayor to get down there now, or else this was going to get really ugly. We were ready to take over Greenwich Village.

I jumped down off the cop car and screamed at the top of my lungs, "Gay power!!" Elation rose from my stomach and into my heart. For the first time in my life, I was proud to be gay. My brothers and sisters were all around me. People were shoulder to shoulder, arm in arm, screaming at the cops and throwing stones, chairs, bottles, and sticks. We had the high ground, we had the moral outrage, and the power was with us. We started chanting again, demanding that the mayor face us. "Gay power! Gay power!" the crowd called out.

More cops arrived. They jumped out of the cars and started to circle the park. One of my friends grabbed me and dragged me down a side street, away from the melee. As I stumbled into the darkened street, the sounds of the riot faded into the background, and I felt suddenly exhausted and afraid. My chest heaved. I was unable to catch my breath. I tried to gather myself as I continued to hurry away from the battle. Soon, I realized that I was safe. My breathing was fast and my heart was pounding, but under control. Jubilation rose within me and exploded into laughter and joy. My friend and I started to playfully smack each other's shoulders and then we threw our arms around each other as we walked down the street. Pride in who I was and what I had participated in filled every cell of my body. I was a freedom fighter!

That night, which came to be known as the Stonewall Rebellion, gave birth to the Gay Liberation movement. It changed the entire country and a great deal of the world. For three more nights, gay men and women demonstrated outside the Stonewall Inn. Many showed up in drag as an overt way of demonstrating their homosexuality, but, contrary to later accounts, there were no drag queens on that first night. On that night, ordinary gay men and lesbian women were just minding their own business and trying to have a good time—until they were told that they couldn't.

In the weeks that followed, New York was radically transformed. Gay and lesbian people had found their voices and their power, and were ready to organize. The Gay Liberation Front, the Gay Activists Alliance, and eventually the Human Rights Campaign were born, and immediately, these organizations began investigating ongoing police abuse of homosexuals and of business establishments owned by homosexuals. Soon, the depth of police bias and brutality was revealed. Although it was not against the law for bars to serve liquor to gays, the police routinely raided bars that did. The police also shut down bars that allowed people of the same sex to kiss, hold hands, or wear clothing associated with the opposite sex. People of the same sex were not allowed to dance together in public, according to the police, and bars that allowed same-sex dancing were subjected to regular raids. These were just some of the unwritten but widely accepted rules that allowed the police to take away the rights of gay men and women, and shut down the places they frequented. Even though we all knew this to be true, we felt very different when this information was brought into the light of day. We soon wondered how we had accepted these things for so long. What had we been thinking?

Similar transformations occurred for gay men and women throughout the country and around the world. Soon, the Gay Liberation Front pressed state legislatures and Congress to provide legal protection for gay and lesbian people nationwide. Similar organizations sprang up in Canada, Great Britain, France, Germany, Belgium, the Netherlands, Australia, and New Zealand. June 28, 1969 had changed the world—and me with it. Suddenly, all the rage that I had turned against myself was focused outward for a just cause. Something shifted inside of me. I couldn't immediately make sense of what it was, but I knew I was different. I felt a new power within me, a power that could change my life.

6

The Golden Goose Lands at the El Monaco

Just after noon on July 15, 1969, I hurried out of the motel office to the grass-covered front yard and arranged a series of white sheets on the ground to form a large cross. Momma looked on in horror, expecting that at any minute, I would strike up a revival meeting. She put her hands to her cheeks and screamed, "He's putting a cross on mine lawn? *Oy gettenu!* (Oh God!) And with the good sheets! Mine clean sheets!"

I looked to the horizon and waited, barely breathing. The sky was clear, the sun was out, the omens were good. The Earthlight Players, the acting troupe that I had brought to the El Monaco, were singing and dancing in the background, celebrating what they thought would be the answer to all our prayers. To Momma's horror, they had stripped off all their clothes and painted their bodies with lipstick and mud, apparently giving in to some kind of atavistic impulse. For me, the world had stopped; all was still despite the chaos that surrounded me.

There! There it is! I said to myself. A dot had appeared on the horizon and was getting bigger by the instant. And then, as if in confirmation, I heard the soft *whump, whump, whump* of the helicopter blades. Initially, the sound was so faint that I couldn't tell if it was the bird or my beating heart. But now I could clearly see the outline of the helicopter and hear the sound of its call. It was as if the cavalry were coming to my rescue. Oh, bring money, cavalry, bring money!

In minutes, the great silver and white aircraft was hovering above me, blowing the sheets and everything that wasn't tied down in all directions. I felt the pounding of the wind from its blades, and my mother's screams were drowned out by the beast's thunderous clapping. Even the naked Earthlight actors scattered in the wind. I backed away and watched, as if in a dream, as the helicopter descended from the sky and landed softly in front of our office.

A door slid open and out jumped a young man with long, curly brown hair. He wore a vest, jeans, and flip-flops, but no shirt.

"Elli, is that you? Mike Lang! Good to see you, buddy," he said with a big smile on his face. He held out his hand to grasp mine and then said, "It's been a long time."

I was so stunned that at first I didn't know what to say.

❧ ❧ ❧

That morning, I had read an article in the local newspaper, *The Times Herald-Record*, reporting that the good people of Wallkill—a community just fifty miles to the south—were canceling the proposed Woodstock Music and Arts Festival. The town council rescinded Woodstock's music permit out of fear of what the concert and its patrons would do to the local environment. Woodstock's producer, Michael Lang, had estimated that fifty thousand people would likely show up for the concert. And when Wallkill's town fathers conjured up the image of fifty thousand hippies and assorted drug dealers descending on their fair town, they suddenly panicked. No way, was the official verdict.

The Times Herald reported that concert promoters had already invested about two million dollars in stage structures, sound equipment, water lines, and toilets. Apparently, there were perhaps a hundred trucks and trailers already en route to Wallkill bringing supplies and technical equipment. Hundreds of technicians were standing by. If the promoters didn't find a suitable alternative site within twenty-four hours, they were going to cancel the show entirely. The promoters planned to sue in order to recover their investment.

The concert itself was hardly news to me—it had been a *cause célèbre* in the local newspapers for months. And for just as long, I had been battling the demons that assaulted me, especially at night, when I had time to consider the fact that the universe had conspired, once again, to put the solution to all of my financial problems just out of my reach—oh, say, fifty miles out of reach. I was extremely upset, you might say; so much so that I had started to wonder if my atheism was working against me. Maybe there was a God, and maybe He and Moses were having a big laugh as they dangled me over the fire. "Get that big foot ready, Moses. We're going to turn this matzo ball into matzo flatbread."

But suddenly, it seemed, all of that could change. The Woodstock Music and Arts Festival needed a home and a permit. *I have the permit,* I said to myself. *And I can provide the home.* My brain danced in creative patterns previously reserved for imaginative sex acts and romantic evenings in the Moulin Rouge or New York S&M clubs. Opportunity was knocking on my motel door. *Oh my God! We could host this thing!*

I had been sitting with some of the Earthlight troupe members in our office, and when I was done reading the newspaper article, I picked up the telephone and called Michael Lang.

"Do you know Michael?" a voice on the other end of the line asked.

"No, I don't know him and he doesn't know me," I said. "I'm the president of the Bethel Chamber of Commerce and owner of the El Monaco International Resort in White Lake. I have a valid permit for a music and arts festival, along with fifteen acres of land that Woodstock can have. Immediately, if not sooner."

The line was quiet and for a moment I became aware of the Earthlight actors quivering beside me. Suddenly, Mike Lang was on the phone.

"Where the fuck are you, baby?" he said. "What's the deal?"

"Route 17B. White Lake. I'm about fifty miles up the highway from where you are."

"Do you have a fucking lawn?" he asked.

"Yes, we have a lawn. A big lawn."

"Do you have some white sheets?"

"What? Of course we have sheets. We're a motel."

"Put the fucking white sheets out in a cross on the lawn, baby, and we'll be there in fifteen. I'm looking at the map. You have a landmark there? A sign? Something we can identify from the air?"

I mumbled something about the El Monaco's sign, the Route 55 intersection, Yenta's Pancake House.

"We're on our way, baby," Mike Lang said, as he hung up.

For years, I had been hoping for something big to happen, and now I was trembling like a leaf. I hung up the phone and was greeted by a spontaneous cheer from the Earthlight Players, who had been listening to every word of the conversation. If a big concert was coming to White Lake, it had to mean something good for a troupe of actors, too, they reasoned. Now they were jumping up and down all around me. "We knew you could do it, Elliot," one of them said. "You're the man!"

With that, they ran out onto the front lawn and began dancing in celebration. And then they did the only thing they could think of to make Mike Lang feel really welcome; they stripped off their clothes and danced around in their birthday suits. As they danced, they passed around lipstick and handfuls of mud and painted peace signs and words of love on their bodies.

Ignoring the chaos, I got some sheets from a closet in the office and raced out to the lawn, where I arranged them in the shape of a cross, as advised.

When the helicopter hovered above us, blowing everything out of its way, it occurred to me that this kind of entrance was reserved for mythic heroes. The ordinary person doesn't just order up a helicopter to carry him a few dozen miles up the New York State Thruway. No, Homer himself could not have conjured up something more elaborate, nor more appropriate, for the man who jumped out of the fuselage and was now walking toward me.

Right behind Mike walked a petite young woman, whom I was about to learn was Lang's assistant, Penny. In Penny's arms was a tiny Yorkshire terrier that seemed quite at home in all of the mayhem. And right behind Penny came two very hip looking men, who didn't bother to introduce themselves. All three approached me, with Lang out front, his hand extended.

After his initial greeting, Mike Lang said, "Don't you remember me, Elli?" I was thrown for a second because only my family called me by that name.

"Do we know each other?" I asked.

"Bensonhurst! Seventy-Third Street," Lang said. "We grew up together. I lived across the street from you! We played stickball together. I'm Mike Lang," he said again. "You're Elli Teichberg."

Someone would later describe Mike Lang as a cosmic pixie, which wasn't far off. In addition to the curly hair, which fell all the way to his shoulders, he had big, round eyes that were brightly lit, round cheeks with dimples, and a wide mouth that turned upwards in a smile, as if he were constantly amused.

There was an air about Mike that was both playful and deadly serious. From all outward appearances, he was a hippie. Yet, I could not deny that he had a certain gravity, like a man who was more than what he appeared to be.

For the life of me, I could not remember Mike Lang, or even playing stickball, for that matter. Even more mysterious was how he connected Elliot Tiber, the name I had given him, to Eliyahu Teichberg of Bensonhurst, especially since I had not mentioned Teichberg or Bensonhurst. And how had he done this in the space of fifteen minutes?

We went into my bar—the Earthlight Players still dancing all around us—and Lang asked to see the festival permit. I handed it to him. It stated that Elliot Tiber, of the El Monaco Motel, has been granted permission by the Bethel Chamber of Commerce to hold a music and arts festival in White Lake during 1969. I told him that I was president of the Bethel Chamber of Commerce and would gladly assure the cooperation of the local business community so that a repeat of the Wallkill debacle would not occur.

"Permit looks good," Lang said. "Let's have a look at the land."

As we left the bar, three stretch limousines arrived with more Woodstock people, including Stan Goldstein, the Woodstock security chief. Goldstein was a serious guy—tall and lean, with dark hair, dark skin, and skeptical eyes. He didn't smile when he shook my hand.

I escorted Lang and his entire group through the fifteen acres of swampy land, passing my White Lake Summer Barn Playhouse, cesspool, and a dozen naked Earthlight Players, some of whom danced around the helicopter. Momma tried to cover them up, but they refused her *shmattas* (rags). Unfazed, Momma tried renting chairs to passersby who stopped to witness the commotion and watch the crazy naked dancers. "It's a preview of their dance performance," Momma told them. "What do you think, darling, they dance for free?"

The ground was soaking wet. We started passing some of my signs, which were posted throughout the motel grounds. We passed the "Jerry Lewis Wing," and then the "Presidential Wing, formerly the Moulin Rouge Wing." People looked at the signs but said nothing.

The day had inexplicably turned cloudy and cool, but I was sweating profusely. Lang had stopped smiling, which I took as a bad sign. Goldstein didn't look happy, either.

We passed the collapsing bungalows and were getting deeper into the swamp. Another sign appeared: "Elvis Presley's Blue Suede Shoes Pool and Cabana Club. For Guests Only. Outsiders Will Be Sent to Prison Forever Unless They Pay the Daily $5 Fee to Sonia the Pool Savant."

I dared not look in their eyes. No doubt they were thinking that I was totally mad. On the other hand, they didn't run in the other direction. They were desperate. I was desperate. This was a shotgun wedding.

"Don't you have any open space?" the beatific Lang asked.

"There's an open meadow-like area just ahead," I explained, trying to remain upbeat. The Woodstock entourage followed behind me, their expressions becoming ever more disappointed with each step. They must have thought I was some Florida shyster trying to sell land under water. Some of them started whispering among themselves. Even the Yorkie seemed mortified.

We passed more signs, including the "International Cultural Information Booth." We passed more buildings—the "Hollywood Palm Plaza," which was the collapsing rooming house in which the Earthlight Players stayed. And as we walked, I began to believe that deteriorating bungalows, soaking swamp, and crazy signs would kill the deal. If that happened, I would promptly set fire to the entire compound and gladly go to prison for arson.

Finally, we were twenty feet from the site. I felt relieved that my sign orgy was over. There was no way I could explain to these strangers, whom I hoped were my saviors, that my sign therapy was one of the things that kept me alive as I waited for the day when they would suddenly appear out of the sky—just as I always dreamed they would.

I hadn't been down at this end of the compound in months, so the huge sign swinging like a hammock between two pines—complete with fake palm leaves that I'd stolen from Lord & Taylor—shocked even me: "Coming Soon on This Site: 200-Story Convention Center, Gambling Casino, Health Spa, and Space for 2000 Cars."

My fragile psyche had been exposed before all of them. All I could do was keep walking and pretend that I was invisible for the moment. I thought it would be a hundred years before we made it to the site, but finally, we approached an open swamp. All of us tried to stand upright as we sank into the sodden and soggy earth, which was, in so many ways, the true foundation of the El Monaco Motel.

Lang turned to Goldstein and said, "Couldn't we get a dozen bulldozers in here and level it? He's got a permit! He owns the land. He's the president of the C.O.C.!" Goldstein immediately vetoed the idea. Draining the ground was impossible. There simply wasn't enough time to get it ready.

In the background, I could hear more whispering among the entourage, and the tone wasn't good. I could see that everything was falling apart before my eyes. I knew that this was my last chance to save the motel and myself from eternal damnation in White Lake.

I panicked and made a variety of pitches that included hanging a stadium from sky-hooks and filling the entire El Monaco compound with cement that would be dry by the time the concert was underway. Perhaps I crossed that thin line of sanity when I told them they could nuke the whole fuckin' place to oblivion and put on the concert atop the ashes.

And then, suddenly, I was inspired. What about Max Yasgur's farm?

"Hey Mike, I have a neighbor who has lots of open space. He has a big farm. Hundreds of acres."

"Where? Who?" he asked.

"Just up the road," I told him. "He's my milk and cheese man. His name is Max Yasgur. He has the best cottage cheese and milk in the county. He's a swell guy. Maybe he'll rent you his farm. He's just got a lot of cows grazing there. There's plenty of space for a concert. In fact, the land slopes in places to create a natural amphitheater. Let me call him."

We all walked back to my dance bar so that I could make my call. Lang and Goldstein were cool and I tried to look cool, too, but suddenly I dropped all pretense and did a Gold Medal sprint through the swamp, past my naked theater troupe, past the cesspool, and straight to our one working telephone.

Once on the phone, I reminded Max of how much he liked my music festivals and how much he did to help me out. "If we can have our music festival on your farm, Max, it would save me from giving the El Monaco to the bank, and my folks from having to take in wash someplace in Miami Beach. I could even triple my milk and sour cream orders. Max? Say you'll do this."

"Sure, Elliot," Max said. "August is so quiet here. You know me, I love music. Come over with your friends and we'll talk."

I got in the Buick and Mike Lang and his entourage got in their limos and followed me to Max's farm. As we drove, the sky turned blue again.

Mike Lang, Goldstein, and the entire entourage went gaga the minute they saw the huge, open acreage of Max Yasgur's farm, with its rolling hills and natural amphitheater. The place was heavenly, no doubt about it, and perfect for a concert.

I led Mike and Goldstein into Max Yasgur's little store next to his farm, and did the introductions.

"Max, these fellows need the land for a three-day concert," I said. "We need to get started tomorrow because the festival is August fifteenth, sixteenth, and seventeenth, and there's so much to do and so little time to do it. Okay?"

Max was forty-nine years old, but he looked older. He had an oval-shaped head, with very little hair on top, and thick glasses with heavy dark rims. He had small eyes, a Jimmy Durante nose, a wide mouth, and ears that stuck out a little bit. His skin was burnt brown after decades of farming in the sun. His body was strong, though, from all the hard work. And the impact of his presence was wise and kind. In fact, Max was a *mensch* (a good person) and it showed. But he was nobody's fool, either.

"Think, Max, you could have the exclusive for supplying milk and cheese and yogurt to ten thousand music lovers!" I said. Max nodded in agreement and smiled, perhaps as much at my desperate efforts to influence him as at the thought of the windfall he was about to enjoy. At that moment, I turned and looked at Lang, whose smile turned into absolute sunshine. I melted. My feet were not going to support me if I didn't have a chocolate egg cream or chocolate milk—Yasgur's chocolate milk. But I stayed cool. I looked cool. I looked hip. Okay, so I didn't look hip. Lang, with his enormous mop of brown curls, was hip enough for everyone.

We decided to go to DeLeo's Italian restaurant, which was on the lake, right across from the El Monaco, and discuss the details over lunch. I knew better than to serve them Momma's stew on paper plates that we'd gotten at a going-out-of-business sale. I did not think this was the moment to show off the motel's facilities and staff, either.

On the way to the restaurant, I considered my options in case the deal fell through. The first order of business was to set the hotel on fire—that much was a given. Then I'd flee to Mexico, or become a sex slave in Bangkok, or start a new life among the Bedouin on the dunes of the Sahara. I also decided to punish God and the whole Jewish race by involving my bar mitzvah *tallis* and *tefillin*—prayer shawl and leather boxes containing scripture passages—in various kinds of sex acts, as yet to be determined. I prayed to the God in whom I didn't believe: *C'mon, don't forsake me now.* That prayer was followed by threats of even greater sacrileges, which I would think of in due course.

When we got to the restaurant and took a table, Max waxed eloquently about my many contributions to White Lake, including music festivals, art shows, theater presentations, and classical music selections. The last contribution was always provided by my Webcor record player in lieu of having performers who knew how to play their instruments—a fact that Max, being the gentleman that he was, neglected to mention.

"You guys are lucky to have Elliot here on your side," Max said. "He has single-handedly brought whatever music and art White Lake has. He's a nice boy. His mother is a nice lady. His father fixed my barn roof, and it never leaked again."

As Max went on, Mike Lang just smiled. He seemed completely genuine. He wasn't hurrying matters or pushing Max to name a dollar figure. On the contrary, he was relaxed, cool, hip—even, dare I say it, respectful.

Finally, Max got to the money end of the conversation.

"Elliot, I know how hard you and your family have worked to keep things going," Max said, and then paused for a moment, thinking. "Would fifty dollars a day for the three days be okay?"

How did he come up with such a figure?, I wondered. Perhaps he looked at Mike, who wasn't wearing a shirt or shoes, and decided that the guy was broke. And, of course, Mike came with me, which didn't boost his image any. As Max had said, my fortunes hung by a very thin thread. So what else could Max think but that I required yet another act of kindness?

"Sure, Max," said Mike, a big smile never leaving his face. "We can do that." With that, Max and Mike shook hands—and I nearly passed out from shock. The Teichberg Curse hadn't screwed up the deal despite the fact that we were eating *traife* (nonkosher food). On the other hand, we weren't out of the restaurant yet.

We paid the check and as we passed the cash register near the door, we heard a radio announce the news at White Lake.

"This just in," said the voice on the radio. "Mike Lang, producer of the Woodstock festival, is meeting at DeLeo's Restaurant in White Lake with Elliot Tiber of the El Monaco Motel and Max Yasgur of Yasgur's Dairy Farm. They are discussing plans to move the Woodstock festival to White Lake."

The three of us looked at one another. Max smiled. Mike smiled. I tried to smile, but at the same time, I wanted to run back to the table and take back the tip that we had left the waitress, who had obviously leaked the story. Now I was *really* afraid that Max would pull out of the deal.

Max got into his truck and drove away, but once he was gone, I assured Mike that there were other farmers who would provide us with the land if Max pulled out.

"Don't worry," said Mike. "It's cool."

The minute we got back to the El Monaco, the phone rang. When I heard Max's voice on the other end of the line, my heart started racing in fear. Max said he'd made some calls and learned that there might be as many as fifteen to twenty thousand people attending the festival. He'd be delighted to host the festival, Max assured me, but he now wanted five thousand dollars a day.

"It'll cost to restore my farm after fifteen thousand people stomp all over it, Elliot," Max said. "Don't worry, Elliot. I won't screw your festival. Trust me."

It wasn't a matter of trust. I liked Max a lot, but he didn't know that the two of us were up against the Teichberg Curse, which was now working overtime to destroy this entire project.

I relayed Max's new demands to Mike. He was still smiling.

"It's okay, cool," said Mike. "I can live with that. I have to talk to some people, but it'll be a go," he said.

The next morning, the Teichberg Curse was up at dawn. The local radio station and newspapers reported that fifty thousand tickets had already been sold to the festival. Speculations were being made about the damage that might be done to the community if that many people showed up for a rock concert.

Right on cue, Max telephoned me and raised his price again, this time to fifty thousand dollars for three days. He also demanded little add-ons such as cleanup guarantees, health and medical facilities, and insurance. In 1969, fifty thousand dollars was about half a million dollars in today's money.

I nearly passed out from a combination of fear and grief, certain that all was lost. The Teichberg Curse had pushed me to my limits and was about to send me over the edge. When I relayed Max's latest set of demands to Mike Lang, Mike said, "Yes, Yes, Yes. Why so worried? C'mon, babe. Whatever it is, no problem. We can deal with it."

And deal he did. That day, I stood in terror and awe as Mike and Max made the final arrangements and signed a letter stating that the Woodstock Music and Arts Festival would be performed on Max Yasgur's farm. I had never witnessed a handler like Mike Lang. In the marketing fields I moved in, the big guys in big suits crunching big numbers at Macy's and Bloomingdale's were pale next to Mike Lang's hot pink neon light. He knew the numbers, the demands to which he should comply, and concessions that could not be made. And all the while, he never seemed impatient, pressed, or anything but cool. When Max and Mike shook hands, I wanted to kiss them both—out of gratitude, to be sure, but also from sheer relief.

That night, the word went out to the newspapers, radio stations, and television news programs. It was official: The Woodstock Music and Arts Festival would be relocated from Wallkill to Bethel. The show would go on, and the Teichberg Curse had been lifted.

7

The World
Is Made Anew

The following morning, the sixteenth of July, I drove over to Newman's Drug Store in Bethel to have my favorite item on the menu: egg salad and bacon on toast. Still groggy from the events of the previous day, I ordered my sandwich and picked up the local newspapers without giving thought to my immediate surroundings—until I realized that everyone in the place was staring at me, many with shocked expressions on their faces.

My eyes went from the faces in the diner to the newspaper and a full-page ad that said, "To ensure three days of peace and music, we have left Wallkill and are now in White Lake, New York." The ad went on to explain that political disputes had forced the move to White Lake, but that the new site offered twice the space, which meant that even more people could attend the festival. It concluded with, "See you at White Lake for the first Aquarian Exposition"—the original name for the festival—"August 15, 16, and 17."

The newspaper shook in my hands. I looked up at the crowd, and as if on cue, an angry man started yelling at me. "You did this, Teichberg! Who needs these fuckin' drug and sex perverts? We'll get you. And don't worry, your fucking motel won't be there much longer."

Suddenly, the diner exploded with voices. Curses and threats were hurled at me with wild fury. At the same time, a smaller chorus of voices spoke up in my defense. Perhaps a little in shock, I looked down again at the newspaper, almost oblivious to the disorder breaking out, and realized that I had just baked the biggest apple pie of my life and that everything else—including this hysterical rabble—was just Greek chorus.

With that realization, something like nirvana overtook me. Without a shred of fear, I paid for my sandwich and walked out to the Buick, the mob of detractors and supporters surrounding me like a hurricane around its eye. Some wailed with lamentations and threats to my life. "You Jew bastard. You think we're going to stand by and let you ruin this town? We'll run you out and all those dirty hippies with you before we let this happen."

Not everyone saw me as the devil, however. Esther Miller, a woman in her seventies—or maybe her nineties, I never could tell—was walking by my side as I approached my car. White-haired and wrinkled, Esther owned an old, dilapidated hotel on the square with thirty rooms, only a few of which were rented each season. Now she grabbed my arm and embraced me. "As of this morning, Elliot, my hotel is fully booked. Thank you. You did this." With that, she turned to the crowd and yelled, "Ruin this town? Elliot just saved us, you fools!"

Al Hicks, a local grocery store owner, shook my hand. "This is the first good thing that's happened here in fifty years," Al said.

The yea-sayers did not have much of an effect on my detractors, though.

"Do you know what fifty thousand hippies are going to do to this town?" a man yelled out. "They'll level it. They'll be high on drugs—robbing us during the day and raping the cattle at night."

I opened the door to the Buick and slid into the driver's seat, the mob screaming at the back of my head. They pounded on the windows of the car. Many kept repeating, "We'll get you and your crazy parents. You hear us, Teichberg? You hear us?"

It was a good question. Some part of me was cautiously recording the events, but another was entertaining fantasies. Finally, more than a decade of hope was about to be fulfilled. I had been living in a tourist town that had no tourists, and nothing to attract them, either. Bethel's only claim to fame was its history as a burial ground for the mob. Back in the 1920s, mob bosses would bump off former colleagues in Queens or Brooklyn, take the two-hour drive up the New York State Thruway, and dump the bodies in White Lake, where they never would be found. This was the place where both the living and the dead came to disappear. Now the town was going to be resuscitated by the biggest party in the world.

But I was also vaguely aware that calling Mike Lang and actually bringing the concert to Bethel was slightly out of the normal range of my character. Suddenly, I had assumed a higher profile than I was accustomed to. Yes, I did my little music festivals, but they were under the radar—far under the radar, like invisible. People who did big things—Mark Rothko, Tennessee Williams, and Truman Capote, for example—were in another universe. I was not equal to them. *What had changed?* I wondered. Was it Stonewall? Was it the fact that at a new and deeper level, at the level of my rage and guts, I had come out? Clearly, I wasn't hiding as much these days. Perhaps that was having a bigger effect on me than I had realized.

Of course, my doubts were never far from my conscious mind. As I drove back to the motel, the buzz wore off a bit and the enormity of the drug store incident started to hit home. Perhaps the crowd was right. Maybe this could get really ugly. White Lake had never seen fifty thousand people before. With that many people, there was bound to be trouble. What would happen if there was a stampede?

Fortunately, I didn't have time to panic. The minute I pulled the Buick into my driveway, I realized that we had passed the point of no return. The parking lot was packed with cars, limousines, and tractor trailers—and more vehicles were pulling in as I entered the lot. Mike Lang had called forth his army, and it was arriving in full force. The sheer number of cars and trucks parked in my lot was both exhilarating and a little frightening. The lot had never been full before, and now that it was, a revelation hit me like a big bag of cement: *This thing has a life of its own, and it's way too powerful for me to control.*

And then I saw a vision of pure courage and glee. In the middle of the parking lot, amid all the chaos, Pop stood like a fearless matador directing traffic to various parts of the property. His big roofer hands were pointing first in this direction, then in that one. He was ordering screaming trucks and fancy cars around like they were his employees. Dressed in his customary overalls, which were permanently stained with tar, and a short-sleeve shirt that revealed his powerful arms, he was the quintessential blue collar worker who had suddenly been made king. I could tell that he was in his glory. After a lifetime of frustration and failure, he was ready for the big dance, and it didn't matter what trouble might lie ahead.

This was his hurrah, too—maybe his last one, I thought, considering his poor health. And he had the guts to walk it like a man.

Inside our little office, Momma was handling the phone with all the aplomb of a frustrated actor who had finally found her spotlight. Calls requesting reservations were now nonstop. Momma filled out registration forms, which had never been used before. Meanwhile, she fielded questions in her all-too-familiar style.

"Darling, we don't know from credit cards. . . . We don't reserve no rooms with air conditioning. . . . Some rooms have running water, some not. . . . Listen, darling, this is no good time to talk. . . . You come, we find a place for you, eh? . . . No, don't send checks. Just send cash. How much? Send two hundred and we work something out."

No sooner had she hung up than the phone rang again. I lifted the receiver, hung up on the party waiting, and handed the phone to Mike Lang. "Hang up on any incoming calls that interfere with your high-wire juggling act, Mike," I told him.

Lang made a few calls and within a couple of hours, the phone company had a small army of trucks and tech people on the grounds, installing the banks of telephones that Lang and his people needed. They also put up a pay phone and booth on the property, something I had been trying to get them to do for the past three years without success.

Outside the office, perhaps a hundred Woodstock crew, technicians, food management people, and waste management people were already trying to find accommodations on the property. And more were on the way.

For the first time ever, the El Monaco was fully booked. Momma stood at the front desk taking money and handing out keys, even though none of the keys matched the locks. "You try it, darling," she told people. "Maybe it works, maybe it doesn't. Who knows?" And with that, she waved them off.

"No Vacancy" was our new permanent status.

Meanwhile, helicopters continued to come and go. I abandoned the use of sheets—they were too valuable now—and instead, set up a landing site using whitewashed stones and boards. Soon, a parade of limousines, Porsches, Corvettes, and motorcycles—all carrying Woodstock staff members—began rumbling into town. White Lake hadn't seen so many fancy cars since the 1920s when bootleggers and Mafia capos regularly came to town.

❧   ❧   ❧

Later that day, Mike Lang asked me to sit down with him in the dance bar and talk about room accommodations for the Woodstock people. When I got to the bar, Lang was already there, sitting at a long table with Stan Goldstein, security chief for the concert; two men I didn't recognize; and a few of Lang's assistants.

Mike made the introductions. "Elliot, these are my partners, John Roberts and Joel Rosenman." Both shook my hand.

John Roberts, then twenty-six years old, was clean-cut with a wide smile, dark brown hair, and a preppy look. He was a little self-conscious and seemed cautious. He didn't look like he'd ever been a hippie, and clearly wasn't one now. Although a young man, he was mature and a little distant, too. I had already read about him in the newspaper and knew that he was the money behind the concert. Heir to a drugstore and toothpaste-manufacturing fortune, Roberts had graduated from the University of Pennsylvania and had served as a lieutenant in the Army.

Joel Rosenman, on the other hand, was instantly impressive. He had dark hair, dark eyes, a prominent nose, a wide smile, and a big mustache that reminded me a little of a Mexican *bandito*. Like Roberts, Rosenman was an Ivy Leaguer, having graduated from Yale. He was raised on Long Island, the son of a prominent orthodontist. As a kid, he learned to play guitar and, after Yale, had toured the country with a rock 'n' roll band. In the process, he had shed the preppy image for that of the hipster guitar player, but he still looked like power and money to me.

"I read about you guys in the newspaper," I said. "So this is the situation comedy that you finally came up with?" Everyone at the table laughed and loosened up a bit.

Roberts and Rosenman had met on a golf course in the autumn of 1966 and, a year later, shared an apartment in Manhattan. Neither had any idea what he wanted to do with his life, but Roberts could bankroll anything that sounded good. By 1968, they had decided to create a television sitcom about two men with "more money than brains," as Rosenman put it. The two characters would get into a new business venture each week, make a mess of things, and then get rescued from their own incompetence at the last minute. It was a program I certainly could have related to, if not starred in.

In order to get ideas for their program, they put ads in *The Wall Street Journal* and *The New York Times* that made an unusual pitch: "Young men with unlimited capital looking for interesting, legitimate investment opportunities and business propositions." They received thousands of replies, including a scheme for making biodegradable golf balls.

"Obviously, the show had some autobiographical roots," Rosenman said. "We sort of became characters in our own show."

Two of the people who approached Roberts and Rosenman were Artie Kornfeld and Mike Lang. Kornfeld, then twenty-five years old, was vice president at Capitol Records—he was only twenty-one when he got the gig, making him the youngest vice president in Capitol's history. He was famous for smoking hash in his office and for writing thirty hit pop songs, including "Dead Man's Curve" for Jan & Dean, and "The Pied Piper," which was a number-one hit for Crispian St. Peters in 1964. As a bigwig in records, Kornfeld had connections with most of the successful rock groups.

Mike Lang had fled Brooklyn as a teenager and opened a head shop in Florida. Later, he produced one of the biggest rock concerts ever staged, a two-day event known as the Miami Pop Festival, which attracted forty thousand people. In addition to his work as a promoter, Lang managed a rock group called Train, for which he wanted to get a record deal. He targeted Kornfeld as the exec to whom he would pitch his group.

Funny, Mike had used the same approach with Kornfeld, whom he didn't know, that he used with me. Kornfeld had grown up in Bensonhurst, as Mike and I had, and when Mike sought an appointment with him, he had Kornfeld's secretary tell her boss that Lang was "from the neighborhood." The two met and instantly hit it off. Few people could resist Mike Lang's angelic charm, and it wasn't long before he was living with Kornfeld and his wife, Linda, in their New York City apartment.

As Lang and Kornfeld explained, the two had an idea to create a huge rock concert and cultural extravaganza in the town of Woodstock, New York. They chose Woodstock because a number of famous musicians—including Bob Dylan, Jimi Hendrix, The Band, Janis Joplin, and Van Morrison—had relocated to the area as part of the back-to-the-land movement. Lang and Kornfeld wanted to create a state-of-the art studio where they could record these and other artists in the Woodstock area.

The two met with Roberts and Rosenman, who would later say that the concert was their idea, not Lang's and Kornfeld's. According to Roberts, Lang and Kornfeld wanted to create a record studio that would be supported by fundraising parties. It was Roberts and Rosenman who hit upon the concert idea and ran with it. Whatever the truth may be, the four joined forces and created a company named Woodstock Ventures, Inc.

Lang wanted to call the concert the Aquarian Exposition, but eventually the company name was given to the event. Hence, the festival was named Woodstock, causing long-standing confusion over where the concert was actually held.

The boys had travelled a bumpy road. The town fathers of Wallkill had axed the deal after realizing what fifty thousand people might do to their little hamlet. Also, they didn't like the promoter's slogan—"Three Days of Peace and Music"—which they believed would attract antiwar demonstrators. The Woodstock four feared that all was lost. Surely, other neighboring towns and villages would block any attempts to stage the concert for the same reasons. That's when I entered the picture and gave the concert a home.

And now, three of the four Musketeers were sitting in front of me. Roberts and Rosenman wanted to meet me, I assumed, to make sure that their huge landing party had a friendly beachhead. So far, the vibe was good.

Momma brought us bowls of cholent and did her Jewish mother schtick, explaining how Jewish mothers just can't rest until everyone is fed. The little party laughed and said how cute she was, which made me want to gag. And then they dove into the stew. "Wow, like great vegetarian stuff," one of the assistants said. It was on the tip of my tongue to explain what they were eating, but I held back. Chances are, they would figure things out on their own before too long, anyway.

"Elli, what do you want out of all of this?" Mike asked.

"Mike, you put the question perfectly," I said. "I want *out* of all of this! If you could rent my rooms, I could pay the bills and take off for parts unknown after the festival."

"That's it?" he asked, smiling. "That's what you want? You're not going to hold us up for some big numbers?"

I didn't know what to say, so I remained silent.

"You got rooms, we need rooms," Lang continued. "What are your rates? How many rooms do you have? How many people can you accommodate?"

"If you use every square inch of space—not all of them legit rooms, you understand—we could hold two hundred fifty to three hundred people. Of course, if you need more, all of White Lake is empty. In fact, all of Sullivan County is empty. Except, of course, for the big guys like Grossinger's and The Concord."

"Why don't you add up the total amount of money you would need for all your rooms for the rest of the season?"

I got out a pencil and paper and did some quick figuring. Our rates were eight dollars a night for a room, which at that time was a standard rate for a cheap room in the Catskills. I added up the rates for rooms, the bungalows, and the shower-curtain-divided spaces. Then I multiplied the whole thing out to the Labor Day weekend. Before I passed the slip of paper to Mike Lang, I looked at the number, which to me looked huge, relatively speaking. After all, we had never been full before—not for a single day, much less an entire season. Nor had we ever approached that crazy American concept called "profit." We had been struggling along at an astounding one-percent occupancy rate—low enough to be threatened monthly with foreclosure, and nowhere near the seventy-four- to eighty-percent occupancy rates expected at the Hilton, the Marriott, or any other profitable establishment.

I passed the piece of paper to Mike, who looked at it briefly, and passed it on to John and Joel. All three of them looked at me with disbelief. They must have thought I was the village idiot. Money was being tossed around like dirt, and I was acting as if my only goal was to save myself from this month's foreclosure notice. Well, the truth was, that's what I had been doing for the past fourteen years. I had been conditioned like a lab rat—running on a treadmill for so many years that when the scientists finally showed up and told me I could get off the bloody thing, I misunderstood them. I thought they had told me to run faster.

Mike smiled that gentle, compassionate, saintly smile of his. Down deep, he probably felt sorry for me.

"That's cool," he said. "We'll rent all your rooms and curtained spaces. We'll move out a week before the festival because we have to be on-site for the three days. And then you can re-rent the rooms. We'll pay for the whole season, but you can rent out the rooms a second time. Maybe after the festival, a few of us will need to come back to our rooms to wind up stuff. Okay? How about the bar and the coffee shop? We need to feed our staff. And what about the theater and the cinema? We need office space and meeting space. Can we rent those, too?"

I was in shock. "You can have anything you want," I said, dumbfounded. "I'll figure out the numbers later on and give them to you."

Even Momma, who was listening to every word of the conversation, knew enough to be quiet for the first time in her life. I looked over at Pop for an instant and caught the look in his eyes. He beamed with pride as he watched his son make the arrangements for something even he knew would be the single biggest event of our lives.

"Okay, it's done," Mike said. We shook hands in agreement. I did my best to look cool, but the sweat on my brow hinted at the drama that was blowing up inside me. I felt like Cinderella—albeit, the male version—and I was terrified that at any moment, Mike Lang was going to turn into a white mouse and the helicopter he flew in on would suddenly become a pumpkin.

Mike turned to one of his assistants and asked him to fetch a large shopping bag from one of the limousines. A few minutes later, the assistant was back with the bag, which Mike handed to me. I looked inside and saw that it was filled with neatly bundled stacks of cash.

"Take out the entire summer's rental fee now, Elli, because we prefer to pay in advance," Mike said. "Oh, another thing. What about serving as the festival's public relations person for the local community? Could you coordinate the locals, the town officials, and all? We'd really appreciate it. How about another five thousand for that job, too?"

The hits just keep on coming, I thought.

"Yeah, sure, Mike. I could do that," I said. With that, Mike reached into the bag and pulled out another five grand.

I was going to swoon, but somehow clarity took hold of me for an instant.

"Oh, Mike, I have one last important request. Can you hire my troupe of terrific actors, performers, and artists?"

"No problem, man. We'll hire all of them. They can start tomorrow. They can organize improvised performances and help move the musicians throughout the grounds during the festival. It'll be fucking cool. They're all hired. We'll work it all out," Lang said.

"Great, I'll tell them this afternoon," I said. "They're going to be thrilled."

But Mike wasn't through. "That reminds me, Elli," he said. "I know you need to make a mortgage payment, so here's what we'll do. I'll announce that the El Monaco is the only ticket agent for the next two weeks. You'll get all the tickets you can sell and the regular commission. Is that okay?"

"Yeah, Mike, sure," I said. I was already in a state of bliss, and another cherry on top sent me over the moon. Concert ticket sales agent? Why not? Of course, I'd been a colossal failure at selling motel rooms, pancakes, and singles weekends for straights, gays, and lesbians. But what the heck, I could give ticket sales a try.

Needless to say, I had no idea what Mike had just handed me. In the weeks that followed, Mike Lang and company ran newspaper and radio ads all over the tri-state area—New York, Connecticut, and New Jersey—announcing that the exclusive place to buy tickets for the upcoming festival was the El Monaco box office, which, in fact, was our motel registration desk. You would think that they had announced the sale of one-way tickets to Eden. In two weeks, we sold thirty-five thousand dollars worth of tickets—and that was commission alone. In today's dollars, thirty-five grand would be the equivalent of something north of a quarter-million dollars. My folks and I had never seen so much money in our lives. Pop and I kept examining the tickets as if they were enchanted. Are these real, we kept wondering, or are they some form of magic bean? But the people kept buying them.

One of the very first things my folks and I did was pay off the mortgage on the motel. For a family that had been late with monthly payments for the previous fourteen years, this was truly a momentous event.

Meanwhile, the telephone never stopped ringing. Locked, as I was, in the poverty mentality, I had stayed with a single line, even though the Woodstock people had installed dozens of lines for themselves. Secretly, I feared that the whole enterprise was going to collapse at any minute and that the Woodstock people would fold up their tents and go home just as mysteriously as they had arrived. Yes, it might all go away, and then the nurses would come in and restrain me and resume the shock treatments that life had been administering all these years. But while all of this was going on, I let myself be delirious with joy.

During that first week after Mike Lang landed, my entire world went into some kind of weird gyroscopic realignment. All of my brain patterns and perceptions of what was possible in life were suddenly rearranged. They had to be, because the old Elliot Tiber in no way could have handled all that was about to happen.

8

The First Wave

I woke up on Friday, July eighteenth, to the sound of car horns tooting their greetings, voices of people calling out in celebration, and motorcycles revving up their engines. I rolled over in bed, bleary-eyed and half awake. "What's going on?" I asked out loud. I got dressed and walked over to 17B, where I saw the unbelievable. An unbroken chain of humanity was motoring and walking into Bethel. Hundreds of people were on foot, walking next to slowly moving cars. Many people were in vans, and still others rode motorcycles. Some of the vans were elaborately painted in DayGlo colors—every shade of glow-in-the-dark pink, green, orange, and blue. Many of them bore peace signs and antiwar slogans: "Make Love, Not War," "Flower Power," "Free Love," "Encourage Nudity Among Flowers," "Power to the People," "Draft Beer!," "Outlaw

Underwear!," and "The Good Fairy Is Wanted by the FBI." Many of the passing vehicles had brightly colored Sergeant Pepper-like cartoons painted on them. And still others praised the mind-expanding benefits of hallucinogens—"J. Edgar Needs a Hit of Orange Sunshine!"

Everyone was playing music in their cars. The voices of Janis Joplin, Jim Morrison, the Beatles, and Bob Dylan rolled out like waves of unmitigated joy and unabashed freedom from car radios and eight-track cassette players. Long-haired hippies in brightly colored tie-dyed tee-shirts hung out of car windows and waved. The citizens of White Lake gathered along 17B and looked on in utter awe and confusion. "We're here, honey," one woman called out to a White Laker. "Let's go to the party."

From that day onward, people by the thousands arrived in Bethel to attend the Woodstock Music and Arts Festival. The flow of traffic into town—which Pop directed for hours at the corners of Routes 17B and 55—was unlike anything anyone had ever seen, and looked like it might never end. Initially, it was reported that about a thousand people a day were arriving in Bethel, which, if things remained steady, would support the revised projections of anywhere from thirty-five thousand to fifty thousand people at the concert. But the August fifteenth opening was still nearly a month away, and everyone knew that the numbers would jump through the roof as the concert drew near. It was just a question of how many, and for how long.

At the El Monaco, every room and every curtained-off, semi-private, and not-so-private space was rented. Suddenly, money was no problem—a first in my entire life. What we needed now was help, and fortunately, there were able bodies everywhere who wanted to work. I hired twenty people to clean the rooms, do laundry, cook meals, wait tables, tend bar, make sandwiches, and mow the lawn. And even those twenty were stretched to their limits. Meanwhile, old hotels and motels that had closed years before were reopening and taking customers, even if the patrons had to sleep on mattresses that were old and moldy, and the water hadn't yet been turned on. Weeks before the concert began, people started camping out at Max Yasgur's farm. The place was filling up by the day, even as the Woodstock crew worked furiously to install toilets and running water. None of it seemed to matter to the thousands flowing into Bethel. The vast majority of them seemed happy just to be there.

By making me the only ticket source for the biggest concert in the history of the human race, Lang had placed me at the epicenter of some other dimension of humanity, one that I had previously encountered only in newspapers and on television. These people were not the New Yorkers I had been used to dealing with all my life. They weren't materialistic or hungry for fortune or fame. They were indefinable, mostly because they had rejected everything that could be recognized as a path to the great illusion known as the American Dream. They were long-haired, denim-clad, loose-hipped, barefooted, bandanaed, and free. Many had colored their hair in shades of orange, pink, red, green, purple, and blue. A lot of them wore beads, peace symbols, and various other ornaments in their hair and around their necks, wrists, and ankles. Some had unkempt beards, very few of them showered with any regularity, and fewer still cared much for the world's approval. Everyone sang, it seemed, and everyone laughed. I had never heard so much laughter in all of my life.

Of course, much of this singing and laughter was chemically induced. There were drugs everywhere—it was as if marijuana,

THC, and LSD had suddenly been legalized. People openly passed joints around as if they were cookies at a picnic.

A lot of people drove onto our lot looking for directions, and many arrived high, the smell of grass strong on their clothing. They would come into the office, give me a great big smile, and say, "Whashappenin'?" The first few times I heard the greeting, I was momentarily confused. It took me a few minutes to realize that they were stoned and had turned three words into one. "Right," I said, my voice trailing off. "Whashappenin'?"

"Do you know where the El Monaco Motel is?" many of them would ask.

Most who stepped into our office weren't stoned yet, but they were instantly high the minute I handed over the tickets for Woodstock. Many locked eyes with me and tried to make some kind of soul connection, as if we shared a larger view of the world that made us kindred spirits. They held the tickets in the air and said, "Right on, brother," "Thanks, man," "Groovy," "Cool, man," "Far out," "You're blowin' my mind, man." Others hooted and hollered and whirled their partners in a circle. Everyone hugged and kissed everyone else.

And at some point in this long parade of humanity, I recognized the obvious. These people weren't trapped in the duality of straight versus gay. They were free in ways that I hadn't even considered possible. This is not to say that they weren't straight or gay or bisexual, but whatever they might be, or whatever I might be, it was cool. The message that emanated from them was that there is no need to be anything but what you are. Enjoy it, man. Live it. The men had broken free from the Ward Cleaver role models; the women had thrown away June Cleaver's dresses. If a man felt like swishing when he walked, he swished. If a woman felt like being openly sexual, she was. If a man or woman was gay, he or she was openly gay. And to my eyes, the gays were everywhere.

At night, the Woodstockers would gather at my dance bar and drink and celebrate the day's work and the upcoming concert. The jukebox blasted music all night long, and people danced until they decided that their clothes were getting in the way, at which point they slithered off with someone to a room or some remote part of the compound. Zippi McNulty, a volunteer stagehand, looked like a blonde version of Superman. He wasn't hiding the possibility that he might be gay. I was still a bit cautious about approaching any man in White Lake, where I had to be extremely careful if not downright secretive. But staying silent as I watched Zippi move around the room in his tight jeans and tee-shirt was too much to bear. *What the hell,* I told myself.

"Those construction boots you got on do not turn *me* on," I told him. "But if I were a masochist and into tough men in dirty boots, I would beg you to follow me to shack number two to check out my collection of whips, leather slings, and the hooks and chains hanging from the ceiling."

"Lead on, my friend," Zippi replied. "That's music to my ears." Thus began a regular routine in which, night after night, shack number two could be seen dancing around on its stilts until dawn. Zippi wasn't the only guest, though. Woodstock was like some kind of UFO that had landed and released armies of the sexually liberated in the very uptight town of Bethel. I had been suffocating in the closet for fourteen years. Now, Mike Lang had thrown open the closet door and let me loose in a wild party of sex, drugs, and rock 'n' roll.

Bob and Jim were identical twins. Both were Broadway dancers, with all the requisite physical equipment—sleek bodies, beautiful faces, and well-muscled legs that gave them the power to fly. At night, after numerous beers and as many joints as I could provide, Bob and Jim would start dancing, first on the floor, and then on top of the bar. When things got really wild, the two would do a strip tease down to their jockey shorts. God, how they filled out those jockeys. One night, after a lot of booze, marijuana, and some wild dancing, I got Jim aside (or was it Bob?), and said, "If I were a fag, I would love to be the cream filling between you two delicious cookies."

Jim grabbed my face, opened my mouth, and kissed me with all the hunger of a lion. Everyone in the bar broke into applause and howling laughter.

And then, out of the corner of my eye, I could see Momma . . . seeing me! She held her hand to her mouth in shock and her eyes were wide open, filled with the image of what she had just witnessed. I had forgotten that Momma and Pop were waiting tables and tending the cash register in the bar that night. And now, utterly aghast, Momma turned around and ran into the basement. I didn't see her come out again for the rest of the night.

The event registered in my mind, but I was too overcome by lust—and the strength of Jim's grasp on my face—to do anything about it. But in that moment, two worlds suddenly joined—White Lake and Manhattan—and something in the pit of my stomach told me that it was okay.

Right on cue, Bob ran over to me and announced to the crowd, "Give me some of that!" He pulled my face away from Jim and gave me another hungry, open-mouthed kiss. Now the applause and hollering got even louder.

"Pop, cash out for me tonight," I told my father. With that, Jim, Bob, and I danced all the way to shack number two, where we did a night-long routine by Bob Fosse. "Love on Broadway!" I kept calling out with glee.

In New York, I had sex mostly in the dark and often in gay clubs, such as The Mine Shaft. Gays didn't dare flirt or exhibit any overt affection in public, lest they be arrested or, worse, beaten up. Such threats served to keep us locked up inside our own inner closets of fear and shame. But when the Woodstockers arrived, everyone was flirting and coming on to everyone else, including the gays—even in broad daylight.

Hank was about five feet ten, muscular, and black. He was from New Mexico, and when he heard about the concert, he dropped everything, got into his car, and drove directly to Bethel, where he volunteered to work as a stagehand. One day, I was pouring cheap bleach into the pool when Hank approached me and asked if it was cool for him to go for a swim.

"It's cool," I said, but then I gestured to the sign by the pool that said, "Pool rules. No lifeguard. El Monaco not responsible for drowning, children peeing in the pool, or anything else that might happen in this water. Swim at your own risk."

"Doesn't say anything about swimming in the nude," Hank observed.

"Nope, nothing like that on the no-no list," I replied.

Hank dropped his jeans and tee-shirt right there on the side of the pool and cut the water like a blade. *Woof, woof,* I thought, as I watched the water roll off his perfect, shining body.

"The El Monaco gives whole body rub-downs, complete with oil, to every black god swimming naked with water glistening on his strong, hard body," I told Hank as he continued swimming.

Hank stopped swimming and tread water for a moment. Looking up at me, he said, "I don't make it with too many white dudes.

Hmmm." He seemed to be considering the possibility, or maybe just playing me a bit. I wasn't sure.

"My first black rape happened when I was ten," I told him. "But after that, we continued until I was about twelve. It happened in my basement. He was about twenty. How old are you?"

"Black turn you on?" he asked.

"No way," I said. "Well, maybe if I'm forced. Push comes to shove, you doing both. I like it that way."

"Yeah," he said. "I like that, too."

✹　　✹　　✹

The summer of '69 turned run-down, humble shack number two into a love palace. But in between my sexual escapades, other more subtle things were happening that were having a big impact on me, as well. Because of the sudden influx of business, I had all of these workers around me—young people who were very different from those I had interacted with before. Sometimes the simplest conversations surprised me. For one thing, I discovered that many of the people who came to Woodstock had dreams that went beyond anything your average New Yorker thinks about—gay or straight. One day, I had a little chat with a guy named Steve, whom I had hired to do some all-purpose chamber-maiding and maintenance around the grounds. Steve was perhaps twenty-five years old. He was a good-looking kid, friendly and open. We were standing in front of the Presidential Wing after he finished cleaning some rooms.

"What are you going to do when all of this is over?" I asked him.

"I saved up some money and I'm going to buy some land and live on it with my girlfriend," he said.

"Where you gonna do that?" I asked.

"We're looking at places up in the Northeast Kingdom of Vermont, up by St. Johnsbury and some little towns up there. It's real pretty country, and there's some land in the hills in Caledonia County."

"What are you gonna do up there?" I asked.

"Well, we're gonna live, you know. We'll build a little house, make a garden. I can find some work." He smiled a kind of boyish, innocent smile. "We'll have a bunch of kids and live the life, you know?"

"Aren't you going to miss a lot of the stuff that you can do in the city?"

"What stuff?" he asked me. "I grew up in New York City and watched my father work all hours of the day, never home, and when he was home, he was drinking and yelling at my mother and the rest of us. Yeah, he had money, but not much else. I don't want that life. The cities are dying, man, don't you know that?"

"I need the city," I said. "It's the only place I have ever been accepted."

"You gotta accept yourself inside before you can find your place," he said in a way that only a twenty-five-year-old can—straightforward, matter-of-fact, and a little pretentious all at once. Still, it hit me where it hurt.

Each morning for breakfast, the Woodstockers ate whatever Pop was serving in the pancake house before they went off to Max's place to prepare for the concert. Mostly it was English muffins and coffee, but people enjoyed reading the menu. And much to my surprise and delight, they actually got the jokes.

"Hey, Elliot," one of the guys would call out. "I had the Ethel Merman pancakes today. Way too expensive, Elliot, but not bad."

"Love those Barbra Streisand cakes, Elliot," another said. "But I'm feeling a little nasal today, know what I mean?"

People were making good-natured comments about my signs, and many got the fact that they were a necessary outlet for me during all those years of motel madness.

One guy blew my mind when he asked me, only half in jest, "When are we going to get to see *King of Hearts* in your underground cinema, Elliot? I think that would be an appropriate film around here, don't you?"

King of Hearts, released in 1966, was a cult classic about a man who flees the Germans during World War I, only to take refuge in an insane asylum. There, he attempts to free the inmates, but not before he goes a little batty himself. "That one tells the story of my life," I said.

Suddenly, there was life at the El Monaco. This run-down, third-rate motel was the center of the universe. In my gut, I realized that replacing the bouffant-crowned yentas from the Bronx, Brooklyn, and Long Island with these multi-colored hippies, hot and cool, was causing me to be born again. For the first time in my life, I felt that people understood me. They saw who I was. They knew what an underground cinema was; they appreciated the kitsch in the menu at Yenta's Pancake House; they related to feelings of being misunderstood. Here were people who were concerned about the environment and civil rights for all minorities. These people loved music, art, and gentle living. It became apparent that they had aspirations that went beyond just success and making money. I was encouraged by the kindred souls now enveloping me.

One afternoon, just a few days after the announcement of the concert, I drove over to Max Yasgur's farm. The sun was bright and the sky clear, except for a few passing cumulus clouds. Maybe two or three thousand people had already set up camp on the land. Little pup tents had been erected at the periphery of the farm. Cars and vans were parked along its edges, too. People were just hanging out, talking, getting to know one another. Meanwhile, scaffolding was being set up at one end of the farm, where a bandstand and speakers would be placed. There must have been a few hundred people working around the farm, getting it ready for the big concert.

As I drove back from Max's place, I passed White Lake and saw a few dozen people skinny-dipping. People were just relaxing, having fun. I passed lines of cars and motorcycles heading toward Yasgur's farm and the town of Bethel. Looking into the cars, I saw men and women, men and men, women and women. It hit me that there was every kind of human being coming to this concert—husbands, wives, straights, gays, celibates, bi- and tri-sexuals, and cross-dressers. Many smiled at me as I drove by; others waved. I smiled and waved back. A little bit of love was passing back and forth between us. In some place deep in my soul, I had a feeling of comfort and even a little peace. I was part of all of these people, the great sea of humanity. Everyone had come together for three days of music and, if we were lucky, a little love. Maybe, in the end, that's the best any of us can hope for.

I pulled into the El Monaco lot, parked the Buick, and strolled leisurely toward the office, feeling calm and unhurried despite the beehive of activity that surrounded me. One of Mike Lang's young male assistants ran up to me.

"There you are," he said.

"Whashappenin'?" I asked him, happy to be adopting the lingo.

"The natives are getting a little spooked. There are a lot of press people here and more coming. Mike wants you to give a press conference."

"Are you kidding?" I asked.

"No," he said. "You're up, Elliot."

9

White Lake Rebels

The press conference was scheduled for the following afternoon. Given the pressures of facing the press and the fact that I had never been the spokesman for anything—except for my own music festivals, which attracted fewer than a dozen people—I thought it prudent to relax in preparation for the big event. To aid the relaxation process, I smoked, oh, maybe half a dozen joints in rapid succession.

That morning, after I had breakfast and cleaned a dozen toilets, I made a beeline for my dance bar, which was the local stash house for the Woodstock crew and assorted passersby. There I rolled a big daddy and several smaller kiddie joints, and proceeded to do some deep thinking about what I should tell the world via the dignitaries who were about to gather. Nothing came to mind. I hoped the weed would bring inspiration when the time came.

The press conference was held in Yenta's Pancake House. Fortunately for me, only the local press showed up. The big guns were still en route, apparently.

There were perhaps six or seven reporters. Most were from newspapers in Sullivan County, including Bethel, Wallkill, and Monticello. The rest were local radio people. In the back of the room, Mike Lang sat, comfortably dressed as always in jeans, a vest without a shirt, sandals, and a little smile which suggested that all was right with the world.

The first question concerned my permit. "Do you have a legal permit to conduct a concert in White Lake?" one of the reporters asked.

I tried to be dignified, but I could feel the marijuana kicking in and my hold on reality loosening.

"There will be a music and arts festival held here on August fifteenth, sixteenth, and seventeenth," I began. "It's just one more summer festival, part of my ongoing yearly music and arts festivals that have made White Lake the truly international cultural center that it is—evidenced by the fact that you wonderful ladies and gentlemen of the press are here to report on it. I have been proud to be the artistic director of these festivals for the past ten years and hope that. . . ."

The reporter rudely cut me off as I was gaining a head of steam. "Do you have a legal permit to conduct a concert in White Lake?" he asked again. Oh yeah, I hadn't answered his question. *Get a grip,* I told myself.

"Of course," I said. "I'm the president of the Bethel Chamber of Commerce." I tried to recover my dignity. "Would a leading civic leader such as myself go ahead with a festival without the needed permit?" I asked rhetorically.

"Do you realize that police are now estimating that there will be ninety thousand to a hundred thousand people here for this festival? What do your people think one hundred thousand hippies will do to White Lake?"

"My people?" I asked. "Native White Lakians cannot be considered people—mine or anyone else's." Something in the still-functioning part of my brain realized that I had lost all capacity to censor myself.

I began to speculate on the irrelevant nature of press conferences in this humongous universe where things are happening all the time, big things and little things, and that we are all just witnessing these events, like the groovy little one that was happening right now in Yenta's Pancake House, with these sweet little people who were so uptight. I was about to ask if anyone had anything to eat when another of those pesky questions was posed.

"Are you prepared to deal with the sanitation issues that will arise if a hundred thousand people come to this concert? How are you going to feed that many people?" a reporter called out.

"Distinguished ladies and gentlemen of the press. Yours is an honorable profession, second in longevity and honor only to the world's oldest profession, and we all know what that is." With that, I raised my eyebrows, gave a little conspiratorial smile, and chuckled. "Let me make a few things perfectly clear. The festival has rented the El Monaco for the remainder of the season and the motel will function as headquarters and field offices. Since you are all assembled, I'll take this rare opportunity to announce that next year my momma will build a two hundred-story skyscraper with revolving health club and United Nations conference center on the eighty-fifth floor. And you are all invited to inspect the proper press room we'll have available there for occasions such as this one. However, since I've got to make up about thirty more beds and clean a dozen or so toilets, today's conference must end. I bid you all adieu."

The reporters looked at one another with mouths open and eyes wide as I gracefully floated out of the room. *That went rather well,* I told myself. Before I got out the door, I caught a glimpse of Mike Lang smiling and casting me a look of approval.

By the last week of July, the police had increased the estimates of the number of people arriving each day to ten thousand. During certain hours of the day, the police created two lanes for people coming into Bethel on Route 17B. Meanwhile, the crowds at the farm were huge—far bigger than anything we could have imagined. A tent city was taking shape, and a sea of people and colors was fast filling up the eighty acres that Max had set aside for the event.

Right after I held my press conference, the major media networks arrived at the El Monaco. Mike Lang had foreseen their coming and asked me to set aside three rooms for the chief news organizations, ABC, CBS, and NBC. He even paid for them in advance. And sure enough, all three networks pulled up in their heavy trucks, complete with receiving dishes and antennae. They rolled into our parking lot like tanks taking a hill. Soon, they were reporting to the world the unprecedented event that was taking place in White Lake. Of course, that only brought more people and more traffic.

There was no driving through town anymore. People walked to the stores, restaurants, and lake, where they bathed naked and hung out in the sun. People rode on horseback and on motorcycles, scooters, and bicycles. Big crowds were everywhere and hippies seemed to be strolling along every street in town.

Since the El Monaco was both the headquarters for the concert and directly across from the lake, people were constantly coming into our lot and looking for help. Many just needed a safe space to come down off a bad trip. A lot of people wanted drugs, which were being given out free at Yasgur's farm. Others needed directions, and still others needed help finding friends who had arrived separately. But all of it was peaceful.

Still, the sheer number of people arriving in White Lake terrified and enraged many of the locals. They began to show their displeasure with the Teichbergs by committing acts of vandalism, which at first were little more than fraternity pranks. At night, people would come by our place and paint swastikas on the wall of the Presidential Wing. They then started decorating the walls with warm-hearted little phrases such as, "We're going to burn down your motel, you dirty stinking Jews." Each morning, Pop would get out of bed, grab his paint cans and brushes, and whitewash over the previous night's artwork.

Of course, the graffiti was only one of the campaigns that the good people of White Lake launched. Another was the ceaseless stream of verbal assaults, which did not stop until well after the concert had ended and all the hippies had gone home. Among the early Christian soldiers to attack us was Bella Manifelli, a big woman with wire hair curlers surgically implanted in her skull. Bella was a perennial in a nearby rooming house with a window facing the lake. One afternoon, Bella visited our little office—dressed as always in her curlers, housecoat, and slippers—to express her immense displeasure with the El Monaco in general and, more specifically, with me. Bella was not at all pleased with the Teichbergs, and to convey her feelings, she chose to call us a number of names: Communists, kidnappers, liberals, Christ killers, mother fuckers, faggots, bus-pass abusers, and, of course, the worst word in that vast vocabulary of hers, the three-letter special—"Jew."

Bella had connections, she wanted us to know. She had power. She claimed that her son was a big judge in Hoboken who lived next door to Frank Sinatra's cousin.

"I'm calling my son collect if you Jews don't stop this festival! I have connections, I tell you. Ask anybody in White Lake what my word means! It's my last warning! We don't need any more Jews in Sullivan County and we certainly don't need any queers!"

Unfortunately, that wasn't Bella's last word. Nor was it her first. For the previous five years, she had made our bar a regular stop in her weekly itinerary. She'd buy a beer and a hero sandwich, and settle on a barstool near the entrance. With her mouth full of sandwich, she'd bad-mouth anyone who passed by, spitting food when her ire peaked. When she left, her closing speech was always the same: "I am here to witness everything you Jewish hotel owners are up to. Prostitutes in the bar! Prostitutes in the bedrooms! Prostitutes out on Route 17B! Nonstop prostitutes! I'm calling my son the judge who lives next door to Frank Sinatra's cousin. And when I tell him what's going on here at the El Monaco, they'll close you down and burn you up. Why don't you people go back to wherever you came from?"

Bella would then exit to great applause from whoever happened to be in the bar at the time. Then she'd wend her way home, worked up and partially intoxicated.

This time, Bella wanted me to know that my actions would cause immediate consequences if I didn't close down the concert. And true to her word, she managed to afflict us with a plague of inspectors. Suddenly, we had health inspectors, fire inspectors, water inspectors, and air inspectors breathing down our necks. Anyone with a license to inspect anything came knocking at El Monaco's door. The neighbors complained to every authority they could find, accusing us of breaking any minuscule ordinance they could dream up. We were trespassing, we were a fire hazard, we were a morals hazard, we were a health hazard. And most grievous of all, we were the ones who turned all those hippies loose on White Lake. They were swimming naked, fornicating in the water, and, God forbid, washing themselves with soap afterwards. Surely, all of this activity was polluting the water. After a day in the lake, many were going to the movies and many more were loitering in front of the cinema, preventing respectable God-fearing Christians from seeing the films.

At first, we tried to accommodate the inspectors. We had nothing to hide except, of course, the fake air conditioner boxes, the television sets that didn't work, and the little fact that we now housed five hundred people in a motel with a maximum capacity of two hundred. The inspectors wrote us up and demanded immediate changes, including the removal of some three hundred extra hippies. I retorted by threatening legal action, which only brought laughter from the inspectors. Finally, I went to Mike Lang. "Mike, they're driving me crazy. Can we do anything about it?" I asked.

"No problem, Elliot. Relax. We've got everything under control. You just let me know when someone's bothering you and we'll deal with it. You don't have to worry about anything."

And the next thing I knew, all the inspectors stopped coming. None of their cease-and-desist orders was enforced, and none of the guests had to leave the motel. Somehow, Mike had made all of it go away, but how he managed this miracle—one of many—was a mystery to me.

Mike had his ways, to be sure. And one of them, of course, was money, and he had a lot of it.

❉   ❉   ❉

The day after the press conference, Mike came into the bar and asked me to run an errand with him. He was carrying a bulging plastic bag, which he held rather casually, as if it contained nothing important. I had been cleaning up the bar after a night of heavy drinking and drug use by the Woodstockers, myself included, and my mind was the functional equivalent of a wad of Silly Putty. To help me wake up, Mike gave me a peek inside his bag.

"Oh my God," I said, suddenly sober. "Is that all real, or are we into printing the stuff now?"

"No, it's all real," Mike said.

"Okay," I replied, "but don't show my mother what you've got in that bag. She'd sneak into your room at night and smother you in your sleep for a lot less."

"Let's jump on my bike and take a little ride. I need your help," said Mike.

Riding Mike's Harley-Davidson, we motored a short way down Route 17B to the White Lake National Bank. It was Friday, and inside, about a dozen locals, most of them farmers, waited on line to cash their weekly paychecks. I was wearing a black shirt and black jeans. Mike, as usual, was shirtless and wearing only a fringed vest, faded blue jeans, and sandals. In addition, of course, was his hair—an unruly mop of brown ringlets cascading down his face and onto his shoulders.

The minute we came in, every head turned and every pair of eyes focused on Lang—his bare chest, his long hair, his sandaled feet. I could see the revulsion in their faces.

The bank's president, Scott Peterson, a puffy man in a seersucker suit, spotted Lang and immediately hurried out of his office and over to us—a move that management consultants in the 1980s and '90s would call "damage control." Suddenly, the farmers, who had been frozen in line, thawed and started mumbling: "Filthy hippies. Drug trash faggots. We'll get you Tiber, and Yasgur, too." Max, who had clearly joined the other side, was going to have his hands full when all of this was over.

I looked at the assembled townsfolk waiting in line and cringed. Lang, unfazed and unafraid, smiled at everyone. Scott was clearly upset by our presence. His face was red and his eyes darted nervously between his bread-and-butter customers and the two oddballs who had suddenly appeared in his otherwise sedate and very proper establishment.

"Can I help you?" Scott asked Mike.

"We'd like to open an account," Mike said.

"We're not doing. . . . " Scott caught himself in mid-sentence, took a deep breath, and then turned to me and said, "Can I talk to you in private?"

Scott ushered me into his office door and said, "We've been doing business with your family for fourteen years. The bank took an ad out in one of your theater programs. The bank helped defend your movie house when the Mother's Committee attacked it. The bank even bought your painting of White Lake—despite the consensus that it doesn't look like any lake anybody had ever seen before—and hung it in our lobby. We try to help your customers. But this is going too far. I don't own this bank. I'm only president of this branch. I have bosses that I work for and they have standards. We don't deal with subversives. Do you understand me, Elliot?"

I glanced over at Lang, who motioned me to come over to him. As I approached, he whispered, "Tell this dude I have two hundred and fifty thousand dollars in cash in my shopping bag."

I ran back to the bank president, who was working up the nerve to throw us both out. "Scott, my associate, Mr. Lang, would like to open an account and deposit the two hundred and fifty thousand dollars he has in his shopping bag." Lang tilted the bag toward Scott and opened it just enough for the banker to glimpse the stacks of green bills inside.

Scott's eyes widened. He walked quickly over to Lang. Suddenly polite and chastened, Scott said, "Can I look in that bag again, sir?"

Lang opened the bag and Scott peeked inside. "With your permission?" he said to Lang. Mike nodded.

Scott lifted out a packet of fifty-dollar bills, pulled one out from the stack, and held it up to the light. His hand trembled, causing the bill to flutter like Old Glory in the wind.

Suddenly stern of face, Scott turned toward the assembled farmers and other assorted locals and shouted, "The bank is closed immediately and will reopen at two this afternoon. Everyone out, please. Now!" He walked purposefully toward the dozen or so farmers who, shocked by what they were hearing, were still standing in line. Taking them by the arm, one by one, he escorted them out of the bank.

"What's going on, Scott?" they protested. "We gotta have our money."

"Come back in a couple of hours and we'll cash your checks," he told them. With that, Scott literally pushed them out the door, locking it behind them. He then took a breath, straightened his suit, and hurried over to Lang, his hand extended.

"I'm Scott Peterson, president of White Lake National Bank," he said. "How can I help you, Mister . . . ?"

"Lang," Mike said. "Mike Lang," now more than a little amused.

Scott ushered us into his office and asked Mike what the bank could do for him. Mike explained that he wanted to open several accounts, including check cashing and payroll accounts for the Woodstock staffers. The Woodstock business management and account team would follow up tomorrow, he said. Hearing this, Scott blanched.

"Tomorrow is Saturday," he said. "The bank is, of course, closed on Saturday."

Mike turned to me and said, "Elli, isn't there a bank in Monticello? That's only fifteen minutes away, right man?"

Suddenly flustered, Scott sprang into action. He grabbed the telephone, dialed the bank's headquarters, and immediately asked for someone whom I assumed was upper management. "No, this is important, goddamnit," he told the person at the other end of the line. "I've got Tiber here from the El Monaco with the Woodstock people. They want to open accounts and set up a payroll system tomorrow. Yes, I know tomorrow is Saturday, you dope. We have two hundred and fifty thousand dollars in cash here for an initial deposit. Yes, it's the El Monaco. No, not the bankrupt El Monaco account. He's *with* the El Monaco. Okay, get back to me."

Hanging the phone up, Scott turned to Mike and asked sweetly, "Are you guys a corporation? What is this cash? Where did all of this wonderful cash come from?"

Mike interrupted Scott with his beatific smile and a gentle question. "Elli, is this the bank that's been threatening to foreclose the El Monaco?"

"Foreclose?" Scott said, anxiously. "Foreclose? No, no no. We've never thought of foreclosing on the El Monaco. We've been doing business with the El Monaco for twenty years. We're neighbors, Mr. Lang. See that painting on the wall in the lobby? The bank purchased that at the first annual White Lake Music and Arts Festival at the El Monaco Motel."

Suddenly the phone rang and Scott reached for it as if it were life itself. "Yes," he said into the phone. He paused, listening. "Oh, yes," Scott said, pausing again. "Good," he finally said. "Thank you. I'll tell him. Yes, they can all come right here and we'll set up all the accounts they want. I'll take care of everything."

Scott hung up and beamed at Mike Lang. "Good news, Mr. Lang," he said. "We will meet you here tomorrow and take care of all of your needs. Now, if you will please sign some forms, I will get you started and we can make your deposit."

As he handed Mike the forms to sign, Scott prattled on about the extensive banking services that were now at the instant disposal of Woodstock, not to mention his undying respect, admiration, and support for the El Monaco as well as the esteemed Mister Elliot Tiber.

Mike explained that the Woodstock group would be making regular deposits over the next month or so, and would appreciate any security measures that could be taken to ensure the safe transport of those funds.

"We will provide free security for the transportation of your deposits," Scott said. "Just call us and we will meet you. I will escort you myself if need be."

As Scott chattered on and on, Mike was busy reading every word on every sheet that he signed. This was no babe in the woods. Mike knew what was what and which way was up. If he had to balance his Porsche in one hand and Janis Joplin in the other, I was certain he could do it with ease.

For the next thirty days, Scott Peterson honored his word. He and his minions did, indeed, escort large sacks of cash from my dance bar, and then transport them to the White Lake National Bank down Route 17B. And everyone who worked for the bank was all smiles and quick to utter sycophantic greetings when the curly haired Mr. Lang entered the bank.

✳   ✳   ✳

By the first of August, Route 17B had become three lanes, all funneling into White Lake. The state police were permanently stationed at the corner of 17B and 55, and when you looked down the hill, the three lanes of cars seemed to go on forever. Fortunately, everything was still moving, but the crowds were continuing to grow. State police now estimated that at least one hundred thousand people would be in White Lake when the concert opened in two weeks, and the number might well be higher.

The locals were on the brink of panic and the town fathers knew they had to do something. The day after Mike and I visited the bank, I received a telephone call from a Bethel Town Council member, who informed me that the council was thinking about revoking my permit to hold a music and arts festival. If the permit was rescinded, the council would close Woodstock down and send everyone home.

"That would be the stupidest thing you could do," I told him flatly. "You will never get another chance like this to revitalize White Lake, Bethel, and the entire region. We are about to experience the biggest boom this town's economy has ever seen. When this concert is all over, we can get Woodstock Ventures to do an annual festival in White Lake. That means a huge influx of money every year. We can become something like Tanglewood in Massachusetts, or Edinburgh, Scotland. We could have year-round tourist trade, with national attention and respect. It will bring the town back from the dead. We'll be able to raise property values and have a tax base that will provide better schools and improvements in the town's infrastructure. You can beautify the entire region with the money you'll make. Do you realize that you are looking at a way in which every person in this town can get rich?"

"We don't see things that way," he told me. "These dirty hippies are destroying the town. They're having sex in the lake, they're parading around naked out in the open. Next thing you know, women will start getting raped. Then what? People all over town are complaining to the council and demanding we shut this thing down. We've got to do something, and we've got to do it now."

Why is it that the stupidest people alive become politicians? I asked myself. As a born-again pessimist, I did what I usually do in such situations—I panicked. And then I went over to Mike Lang's makeshift office in the Presidential Wing, and told him everything that had just transpired.

Mike listened, smiled, and did not panic. I looked for some trace of concern or despair in his brown eyes, and found only serenity and confidence. He picked up one of his two hundred new working phones at the El Monaco and called his people. While the phone rang, he looked over at me, smiled, and said, "Don't worry, Elli. We knew this was going to happen. We've got it all under control, babe."

Two hours later, a helicopter was whirring over the motel and landing softly in our yard. Out of the bird jumped a team of lawyers, all very well dressed and very New York. One of them was a blonde that was a dead ringer for Faye Dunaway. She was dressed in an elegant black suit, a gold blouse under a short black jacket, and heels that lifted a pair of the most beautiful legs I had ever seen. Her hair was golden, like Faye's; her cheekbones high and vulnerable, like Faye's; and her entire face a visage of beauty and intelligence—like Faye's. The minute she walked up to me and introduced herself, I was in love. Yes, I know—I'm gay. But some people are so beautiful and so charismatic that they send your compass spinning the minute you lay eyes on them. She told me her name—Chloe something. I was too much in a fog when she spoke to remember anything she said. It didn't matter what her name really was. It was Faye Dunaway to me.

We all gathered in Mike's office and went over the strategy. Faye described what her team of attorneys was doing to secure the concert at the county and state levels. Apparently, all the needed permits from higher government agencies had been obtained. Everything was in order and ironclad. We were golden, as far as the legal minds were concerned. Mike went over the strategy for tonight's meeting. He asked me some questions, none of which I remember. What I do remember is fantasizing about how I could get beautiful Faye to run away with me. Oh, and I remember reminding myself, every so often, not to drool on my shirt when I looked at her.

Mike decided who would speak first and what each of us would say if called upon by the council. The lawyers jumped in with their advice and at the end of the hour, we were ready for the town council.

At eight that evening, the attorneys and Lang piled into one of Lang's limos and rode one mile down Route 55 to a schoolhouse in Kauneonga, a section of Bethel named for an American Indian tribe that had been wiped out long ago by the soon-to-be Bethel-ians. I rode separately in the Buick.

This was one of those moments when the respective fates of the El Monaco, my parents, myself, Woodstock, and the residents of White Lake hung in the balance, a moment when a town of crazed citizens was ready to make earrings out of my testicles. And all I could think about was this woman. Me, a gay man. Go figure.

The ride over to the schoolhouse was bumpy, thanks to the ten thousand potholes that marked that little stretch of road. You'd think that this bombed-out highway would be enough to convince the locals of how badly we needed money. But no. What they were most concerned about was what the hippies might do to their lawns and lake, and how helpless they were to protect themselves from the madness.

Driving up to the schoolhouse was like arriving at a football game. The place was surrounded by cars and trucks and hundreds of people trying to get into the meeting. This was not going to be your average Bethel Town Council meeting, where four or five cranky old men showed up to vote "No" on everything except buses with curtains. This was more like a throwback to the days of the Salem witch trials. And guess who the witches were.

"Let's hope we get out of this thing alive tonight," I whispered to Lang.

Out of the crowd of people came a friendly face—Max Yasgur. "Howdy, boys and miss," Max said. "Quite a turnout for our little meeting, eh?"

"It's good to see you, Max," I said.

The cinderblock building was packed from front to back. All of the wooden folding chairs, with their squeaky, rusted hinges, were occupied. People were three deep in the back of the room, along its sides, and halfway up the center aisle. The room's legal limit was perhaps a hundred and fifty, tops, but there must have been two hundred and fifty stuffed into the place and spilling out through the front door and onto the sidewalk and parking lot.

At the front of the room sat the seven members of the town council—six men and one woman—at a table on a raised dais. The men were your average shopkeepers and farmers turned politicians—practical folk, mainly. The woman was your smart secretarial type whose most distinguishing feature was the fact that she had no neck and her head sat directly on the shoulders of her rotund body.

The noise level in the room was painful, especially because the overriding emotion was anger, even rage. When Lang, the attorneys, Max, and I walked into the room, the noise level rose. A mixture of catcalls and cheers went up immediately. Our little group was directed to a table at the front of the room, near the foot of the dais. The lawyers and Mike took out file folders from their briefcases and placed them on the table. I sat there, empty handed and feeling rather naked in front of the hostile crowd. Fortunately, Faye crossed her legs and the room went silent for a moment. It didn't last long, though. In seconds, the roar was back.

I furtively looked around the room and gauged the sentiment. A lot of old townsfolk had come out of the woods for this one— the possibility of a multiple hanging will do that, I thought. There were also a lot of dug-in bigots who didn't want outsiders like hippies and Jews to infiltrate and pollute their little patch of paradise. On the other hand, my spirits were lifted when I realized that there were a lot of good people present, too—people who knew that this was, in fact, a golden opportunity for everyone in the region. Judging by the looks being cast my way, the vote was sixty to forty in favor of an immediate hanging from the tree out front.

I must have been trembling, because Mike looked over at me and told me to be cool. He was cool. The Woodstock people were cool. The problem was that the mob was anything but cool.

Suddenly, the president of the council swung his gavel hard on the table. *Bang, bang, bang,* the gavel fell. "We will now bring this meeting to order," he intoned.

One by one, each council member spoke about the destruction, devastation, and degradation that the Woodstock festival and Elliot Tiber had brought to their fair town. The council president cited a list of laws and ordinances that he claimed had been violated by the Woodstockers and those who had come for the concert. Finally, he called upon the council to vote on whether to rescind Elliot Tiber's music festival and art fair permit. Before the vote could be taken though, the council wanted to hear from the representatives of Woodstock Ventures.

At that point, Lang nodded to me, indicating that it was time for me to speak. I asked the council for the floor, the council president nodded his head, and I rose from my seat. I was about to speak when a crowd of hostile voices screamed, "Out of order, out of order!"

Immediately, the friendly half of the room shouted down the unfriendlies. "Let Elliot speak!" they screamed at the hostiles. Before I could get a word out of my mouth, a man in overalls and a five o'clock shadow stood up and called upon Lucifer to curse me and take me to hell. "Visit thy rancor and punish these long-haired demons and give Elliot Tiber a double dose of your most gruesome curses," he said.

A chorus of "amens" followed.

That gave license to one of White Lake's leading ladies to offer the following advice at the top of her lungs: "Exterminate that permit and Elliot Tiber and the Chamber of Commerce with it! Then go out to Yasgur's farm and arrest every single person who isn't a resident."

More "amens" and a lot of "yeahs" followed. They were getting dangerously close to throwing a rope over a thick tree limb, I realized. I tried to gain the council's attention so that I could resume speaking.

Bang, bang, bang, the gavel came down again. "Silence, everyone! Elliot Tiber will be allowed to speak." Again someone shouted that I was out of order, and once more the friendlies told the person to shut up and let me present my case.

I had not had the time or the foresight to run into the bar that day and smoke the entire inventory of hash and marijuana that was stored there. The consequence of that failure was that I was straight—and, therefore, terrified out of my mind. Still, I started strong out of the gate.

"As president of the White Lake and Bethel Chamber of Commerce, and owner of the only motel that is an 'Approved Member' in White Lake, I have been advised by legal counsel that my permit is legal and valid, and that there is no proper legal cause for cancellation of this music festival. I have been running my music and arts festival for almost ten years. . . ."

Upon hearing the legal basis for my permit, the crowd of hostiles began verbally attacking me. Catcalls and shouts rang out. I heard a few graphic threats, but I thought it best—not to mention safest—to turn the other cheek.

When the din died down, I had a burst of inspiration and directed my comments at the town council members.

"What's wrong with you people?" I asked them. "This town is nearly comatose. There's no tourist traffic, no business, no one paying taxes for badly needed town facilities. We're dying! Or haven't you noticed? A golden goose has mysteriously landed on Max Yasgur's farm, with enough golden eggs to feed us all. This Woodstock festival is putting us on the map. We'll have a lot of people coming to our resort town for the next few weeks, maybe fifty thousand or so. (I played down the number as Mike had instructed.) That's fifty thousand live people with cash in their pockets, buying, renting, spending. Maybe this is a one-shot deal. If it is, fine, it's income for all of us. But better yet, maybe this could be a permanent annual festival like Tanglewood and Edinburgh. Every year we could have tourists and income. We could nourish the arts! How can you stand there spitting curses on a miracle! What are you scared of? Long hair and new music?"

That touched a nerve, and instantly the booing and catcalling resumed. I sat down and surrendered the floor to Lang. Wild man Mike Lang introduced himself and coolly outlined how the Woodstock festival was abiding by all the laws of the town, county, and state. He promised to work alongside the community to restore any property damaged by the audience after the festival concluded. And then he uttered a magical sentence: "We will give the town of Bethel twenty-five thousand dollars to be used in any way you deem appropriate after the festival is over."

At the mention of the money, the booing and catcalls briefly subsided. Mike continued speaking, dryly and without emotion. He listed potential benefits of the festival to the entire White Lake and Bethel community. He noted that the festival was building an international telecommunications center at the El Monaco and Yasgur's, and that the music festival would reach audiences around the world. He explained that the publicity would be worth millions of dollars to White Lake, Bethel, and Sullivan County. It would bring new businesses, investors, and tourists, and would trigger a rebirth that most resort towns could only pray for.

The hostile contingent realized that Lang was carrying the day. After he made reference to prayer, hecklers jumped up and drowned him out. "Corruption! Mafia! Commies! Degenerates! Perverts!" they yelled.

At this point, one of the Woodstock lawyers stood up and outlined the legal parameters of the situation. He pointed out that Woodstock had a valid legal permit that gave them specific legal rights. Further, the festival had obtained additional permits from various health and public assembly departments in the county. The festival was meeting sanitation, health, and security requirements. The bottom line was clear. The festival organizers were acting responsibly and legally. In other words, there was no legal argument that could be made against them. And for the smarter members of the Bethel Town Council, this meant that Woodstock Ventures would sue their asses into oblivion if they made any effort to stop the concert.

Finally, Max Yasgur stood up. The room fell silent. Max had that effect on people. He never said much, but his humility and honesty made people take him seriously. Yasgur described his experiences with the festival organizers. They were ethical and straightforward people, he said. They will make good on their promises to the town, and they will be here when the concert is over to make sure that everything is made right. Then he told the crowd that he owned his farm and had a right to lease it as he pleased. There were no laws on the books outlawing or limiting public assembly in White Lake.

Max's legal argument triggered another round of booing and hissing. Suddenly, the mood turned uglier. People started yelling, "Jewish greed! Boycott Yasgur's dairy!" The voices ricocheted off the cinderblock walls. Now things were clearly turning hostile and possibly violent. The town council members sensed the mood, and did their best to bring the meeting under control. The gavel fell again and again, but the catcalls, booing, and name-calling continued. Terrified that a riot might break out, the president of the council told the audience that the meeting was adjourned. The council would reconvene to discuss what to do next, and take a vote on whether Elliot Tiber's permit should be rescinded. "The meeting is closed!" the council president shouted. More screaming and cursing were heard, amid cheers from those who knew the Woodstockers had won.

Lang and the lawyers gathered up their briefcases and walked out of the meeting, the little smile never leaving Mike's face. Outside, Mike turned to me and laughed. He'd never seen such illegal dealings, he told me. "But don't worry, Elli. The concert will go on. They can't stop us, and they know it."

"I hope you're right, Mike. I hope you're right."

10

Everyone Wants a Piece of the Pie

The little body of water known as White Lake is only about half a mile square. Despite its diminutive size, the lake has a curious lore, to which I was about to add.

After the town meeting, hostility against the Woodstock concert rose to a new level. It was clear that key leaders in the Bethel community needed to be encouraged, shall we say, in their enthusiasm for the festival. Soon, several telephone calls were made and meetings were held, all very discreetly. And then one night, someone contacted me and asked me to make a handful of deliveries on the lake after midnight.

White Lake is surrounded by trees and houses with docks and boat launches. On an average summer day, the lake is crowded with boats and the occasional water-skier. But at night, all the boats are gone and the lake becomes quiet and serene. On some nights, mist and fog dance atop the water.

On the Tuesday night following the council meeting, just past the witching hour, I sat in a rowboat at one of the docks and awaited the first of a series of couriers who would arrive at fifteen-minute intervals. As I sat there, shivering in fear if not from cold, I could hear the water lapping up against the side of the boat. Occasionally, a car's headlights would race by, but for the most part, my vigil was deadly silent, save for the crickets and hoot owls that kept watch with me.

Finally, a pair of headlights pulled into a driveway behind the dock. A door opened and then shut. I could hear footsteps approaching and then a dark, menacing figure stood above me on the dock. I had never seen the man before and would never see him again. I nodded, indicating that he had found the right boat. He got into my little dinghy and sat down at the other end, facing me. We made a point of not looking at each other. Neither of us said a word.

Boating lessons were not part of the curriculum at Yeshiva— the closest we got to a boat was the story of Noah—and getting out on the lake was no mean feat. I got one of the oars tangled up in the dock supports and nearly lost it. But finally I got the hang of things and paddled out to the middle of the lake. There I put up my oars and let the boat drift in the dark waters. There was no moon, and the fog and mist coming off the water were thick with the spectral remains of those who had run afoul of the Mafia and now lay at the bottom of the lake. Was I about to join them? Small sounds, like leaves being stepped on, echoed from the darkness of the surrounding woods. I imagined myself being followed by a sniper's rifle. Was my head going to be blown apart at any second? Is that a gun in your pocket, sir, or are you just glad to see me? I wanted to take cover in the bottom of the boat, or throw myself overboard and swim to safety. But I held my mud, at least for the moment.

The mist and fog were too dense for me to see the shoreline, and I guessed that no one could see us, either. If truth be told, I could barely see the hand in front of my face. I reached into a shopping bag that sat at the side of my foot and grabbed a thick business envelope. I handed the envelope to my visitor. He said nothing. I said nothing. No "Thank you very much. Great doing business with you." No "Give my regards to the town council." No friendly inquiries about our respective families, or how the teamsters might be getting along these days.

I rowed back to the dock in silence. As soon as I reached the shore, the man stumbled out of the boat and hurried away.

Sweat suddenly streamed down my armpits and back. *Could I take four more rounds of this insanity?* I asked myself. Right on cue, the second ghost of Woodstock present showed up and gingerly got into the boat. This time, the boat sank deeper into the water and I realized that he was heavier than my first guest. He made his way clumsily to the front of the boat and sat down, facing me. I glanced at him furtively, quickly looked away, and rowed toward the thick gloom at the middle of the lake. When we were out far enough, I reached into the bag, handed a second envelope to my guest, and made haste back to the dock.

When I reached the shore, my passenger stood up and tried to heave himself onto the edge of the dock, nearly capsizing the boat. I held on to both sides of the dinghy and tried to right the thing. Oblivious to my concerns, he tried again, this time sending the boat farther from the dock. "Goddamnit, bring it closer, bring it closer!" he wailed, breathless from his exertions.

I tried to maneuver the boat, but somehow managed to get us even farther from the dock, stretching him perilously between the dock and the rowboat. "I'm going to fall in, you asshole. Get me back, get me back!" he screamed. I grabbed him by the back of his pants, at the belt, and tried to pull him back into the boat. But as I yanked my passenger towards me, the boat moved still farther from the dock and his weight fell forward, causing him to fall face forward into the dark lake.

Half of the man's body was in the boat, the other half submerged in the water, dragging the boat with it. I reached into the water and grabbed the first thing I could get hold of, which was the back of his collar. Desperate, I pulled as hard as I could. Unfortunately, the collar caught the front of his throat, momentarily strangling him. He emerged from the water gagging and making terrifying sounds, like a man being hanged. Suddenly, his shirt ripped open at the buttons and sent him hurtling headlong into the water again, only this time he was out of the boat entirely and completely submerged.

For a second or two, the man disappeared below the dark surface of the water. He then suddenly stood up, the water up to his chest, and cursed me profusely. "You fucking idiot," he said, now wading toward the shoreline. "You godamned fucking idiot. The money's all wet, you fucking idiot." By the time he got to the shore, he seemed to have cooled off. I could be wrong, but I thought I heard him say, "Ugh, I'm getting too old for this," as he climbed out of the water and headed for his car.

"Peace and love, brother," I whispered.

Now I was a nervous wreck. I was ready to leave the bag of envelopes on the dock with a note, "Take one and have a nice life." But the Woodstock dream kept me in the boat.

A third car pulled up. The door opened and closed, and foot-steps hurried toward me.

"Okay, you the guy?" my latest visitor questioned in a whisper.

"Who else would I be at this hour?" I asked him.

"Okay wise guy, take me out there, but stay close to the shore." Again, the stage whisper.

I rowed out a little ways and then turned toward the shore-line. When I felt I was far enough from the dock, I stopped and pulled up my oars.

"What are you doing?" he hissed at me. "Did I tell you to stop? Keep going. Keep going." He was frantic, and the more nervous he got, the more his voice hissed hysterically. In fact, we were more visible from the shoreline than we were in the middle of the lake, where we could hide in the fog.

I rowed farther along the shore. "Where do you want me to go? Isn't this far enough for you?"

"Keep your voice down," he hissed. "People can hear you. No, I don't like this place. Keep going."

This guy had all the makings of a rat—thin, wiry, and nervous. And the farther out we went, the more nervous he became. "Let's go over there," he whispered. I rowed out farther. "Okay," he said. "Stop here. Stop here!"

We were in a cove, canopied with overhanging branches. The boat drifted near a low, grassy outcropping, close to the shore. I pulled up the oars, removed another envelope from my bag, and handed it to my guest.

"Don't hand me that envelope, you moron," he said. "What's wrong with you? Someone could see you do that."

"What would you like me to do, ask one of the fish to deliver it to you? Who's going to see us?" I asked. "We are the only two people within ten miles of this town who aren't stoned blind right now."

Slowly, with a staged deliberateness, he said, "Put . . . the . . . envelope . . . down . . . on . . . the . . . floor . . . of . . . the . . . boat." As he spoke, he tried not to move his lips, as if he were a ventriloquist. "But make sure you keep the envelope dry," he said quickly and nervously. "Now slide it over to me with your foot."

I did as instructed and when he bent down to get the package, I had the urge to kick him in the eye just on general principles.

"Okay, now row back to the dock slowly, like we're just a couple of guys out for a boat ride on a beautiful night."

"Oy vey," I said under my breath. This guy needed a week in shack number two with a pair of pissed-off, leather-clad sados from the Bronx.

The next two trips out to the middle of the lake were uneventful, thank God. When the final man got out of the boat, I waited until I heard his car drive away. Then I hurried to the Buick and drove immediately to the motel bar, where I rolled a very big joint and drew on it until it made me forget all about boats and envelopes and crazy people who hated rock 'n' roll.

☮   ☮   ☮

There must have been something in the air, or in the stars, or maybe people were just getting wind of Mike Lang's garbage bags full of cash. In any case, the next day, a foul wind blew in an old acquaintance of mine, Victor, who used to own a hotel in White Lake. Victor walked into our dance bar and greeted me like we were long lost brothers. He asked for a Tab and I poured him a glass.

Victor was in his mid-fifties, tall, with an overdone tan, silver gray hair, and somewhat sleazy good looks. He had fled White

Lake after making a killing in a land deal that proved to be his undoing—at least locally. A few years before the Woodstock festival, Victor bought some swampland on Route 17B for less than twenty thousand dollars. Coincidentally, the very next day, the town council chose that same swamp as the location for their new sports stadium. Victor was surprised beyond measure, he said. But with luck shining down on him, he quickly sold the swamp for a reported two million dollars. Whatever the profit really was, it was sizeable enough to inspire state officials to investigate the deal and to ban Victor from doing any further business in the state of New York. So Victor hid twenty miles up 17B on the Pennsylvania side of the Delaware River.

Ever slimy, Victor now had a new proposition that he believed was worth risking a border crossing.

"Lots of cars and trucks in the parking lot, Elliot," Victor said as a way to cozy up to me. "Things must be going well for you. How's the whole Woodstock thing going?"

"Good," I told him. "But, as you well know, Victor, you can't please all the people all the time."

"Yeah, well, that's what I want to talk to you about, Elliot. What this guy Lang needs is a liaison team—a couple of guys who can do public relations with the locals, kind of grease the skids so the festival comes off a lot less painfully. You know what I mean? I hear there's a lot of money being thrown around at people. And he needs the help."

A liaison team? I thought I had already been hired to do that, and I told Victor as much.

"Well, what I have in mind is broader, and more lucrative for both of us." Victor explained that a local liaison office was imperative to ensure the continued cooperation of local power brokers.

I started to get nervous. Victor had a way with words. He could make extortion sound like an act of kindness performed by Mother Teresa. And Victor was in his Mother Teresa mode now.

"We could share a fee of, say, twenty-five thousand dollars for being invaluable local coordinators for the Woodstock festival," he said.

"Twenty-five thousand dollars is a lot of money, Victor," I said. "What does Woodstock get for twenty-five grand?" The minute I asked the question, I felt stupid.

With that, Victor showed his fangs.

"Well, you know that permit you have, Elliot? That one, plus the many subsequent permits from various health and safety departments, they all could be voided, revoked, canceled, unless—and this is where you and I could step in—unless Woodstock has a strong liaison team.

"If the Woodstock people don't hire us," Victor said, "I'm sure the local National Guard could be deployed to clear the entire festival site." And with that, Victor finished his tall glass of Tab, flashed his Lucifer-like smile, and excused himself. "I'll be in touch," he said, as he left the bar.

I raced to Lang to tell him of Victor's threat. Lang, ever calm, asked me to arrange a meeting with Victor.

The following morning, Victor, Lang, and a few other festival honchos met in a closed-door session in the graffiti corner of the El Monaco bar. Victor outlined the full range of liaison and public relations services now available to the festival for fifty thousand dollars. My cut was now reduced to ten thousand dollars due to complicated mathematics that took into consideration unforeseen expenses on Victor's part. Some of those complications involved dispensing funds to people in high places in Monticello.

Immediately after Victor's proposal, Lang invited Victor into his private office, now renamed Woodstock Manor. Half an hour later, the two men emerged. Lang seemed withdrawn and thoughtful. Victor seemed livid with rage. I was in the bar, keeping a low profile per instructions from one of the Woodstock people who looked like Walt Disney. Well, he looked to me like Walt, but he sounded a lot like Mel Blanc, and he occasionally quacked like Donald Duck.

Victor stopped on his way out and said, "Elliot, you better advise Lang and his cohorts about the facts of doing business in White Lake. If they think they can cut out our liaison services, they're underestimating Victor. If there is no consulting fee, I guarantee there'll be no Woodstock festival!"

I watched Mike's motel door that morning. Both his Porsche and his Harley were parked in front of his office, which meant that he hadn't gone far. The curtains were closed, but the lights were on and I could hear music playing. Well before noon, a limo arrived and parked next to the Porsche. No one got out of the limo; it just sat there, like some huge beast at rest. Suddenly, Victor drove up to the motel. He got out of his car and nodded to me conspiratorially as if we were in this together. I just looked at him with a blank expression. Mike emerged from his office, accompanied by two business types. Then Mike, the two suits, and Victor all piled into the limo and sped off.

A few hours later, the limo returned. Victor stormed out, made a strange, threatening face at me, got into his car, and burned rubber as he fled. Mike emerged and gave me a victory sign. I hurried over and the two of us hugged. "Everything's cool," Mike said. "Nothing to worry about. We adjusted Victor's nose. Woodstock is going to happen. Relax, babe."

We never heard from Victor again. But the flow of sleaze didn't stop just yet.

❧   ❧   ❧

The next day, a couple of New York gentlemen wearing dark suits and speaking in heavy Italian accents approached me about renting Yenta's Pancake House. They offered two thousand dollars cash for two weeks, or until the festival was over. Yenta's was pulling in maybe sixty to seventy dollars a week, tops. And part of me, I must admit, was still afraid that all the money we were making would evaporate as soon as Woodstock was over. We'd be back in the same place we were before Mike Lang and company arrived—begging for customers, dead broke, and leaking money from every pore and orifice. Up until the time Mike arrived, I had been putting between eight and ten thousand dollars of my salary into the motel each year. Over fourteen years, that's a lot of money, especially in those days. I needed to do everything I could to keep from falling into the same hole we had lived in for far too long. My head said, *Give them Yenta's for two weeks, and get as much money as you can before this Woodstock dream ends.* But my heart and gut told me to be cautious. These were not hippies. These were not respectable businessmen, either. These were dangerous guys whom I should watch carefully. Unfortunately, old habits die hard and my head won out.

"Okay," I said. One guy handed me the cash and we shook hands. I didn't even get anything in writing.

The following day, half a dozen expensive black cars and a couple of trucks pulled up in front of Yenta's and started unpacking boxes of food, beverages, kitchen supplies, dishes—normal restaurant stuff. But then came boxes marked Mexico and others marked Bogota. The guys who were moving the stuff into Yenta's looked like they were right out of central casting for a Chicago gangster movie. They were dark, muscled, and, to get right to the point, scary looking. *What are they doing in there?* I wondered.

I went over to the guy who seemed to be the crew chief—in his mid-fifties, silver haired, and menacing even when he smiled—and said that I wanted to get some of our things out of the restaurant. "No dice," he told me. "We got rights as renters." Pop made the next attempt. He told the guy that he wanted to fix the plumbing problem in the bathroom. "Don't worry about it, we'll fix it," the crew chief said.

I didn't like the feel of things—not at all—and I wondered what these thugs were planning on doing. Selling drugs? Drugs were everywhere—and most of them were free. I went back to the crew chief and said that I wanted to rescind our agreement and that I would give him a full refund.

"Uh, that's not possible," the crew chief said. "Right now, the restaurant is closed because it's being redecorated. If you want to have pancakes, you can go fuck yourself." I asked him very politely if he could come by my office when he was ready and talk to me about the restaurant.

A few hours later, the crew chief and his associate, a Frankenstein type—very tall, very dark, and very thick—came into the office. They made it clear that they had paid in advance for two weeks' rental rights, and that's what they expected to get. Pop insisted that we were responsible for anything that happened on our premises, and said we would inspect the restaurant. They refused to let us do that.

Suddenly it occurred to me that these were not the men with whom I had struck the deal. "Where is the guy I spoke to originally?" I asked.

"Oh, Johnny? He got called to an important executive planning session in Sicily," the crew chief told me. "We bought out his lease. You want to see our bill of sale or what?"

"Johnny?" I asked. "I thought his name was Tommy."

"No. We dunno no Tommy."

I tried to make the case that I had never struck a deal with him and that our agreement was with Tommy. Suddenly, tempers flared and Frankenstein took a swing at Pop. I was no trained fighter and knew nothing about karate or self-defense—I couldn't even climb the ropes at the Midwood High School gym in Flatbush. But I was six feet one and thirty pounds over the top, and used my volume as best I could. I swung at both goons. Then I saw Pop slip to the floor and I went wild. Momma heard the noise and rushed in with Pop's baseball bat. Mom took advantage of her height. At four feet ten, she could swing low, and she took the legs out from under both gangsters. The three of us pummeled the two of them, with Momma doing much of the damage, thanks to Pop's baseball bat. The two ran out of the office cursing.

We called the Bethel police. A couple of storm troopers with crew cuts and mirrored sunglasses came by our office, asked us some questions, and had a short talk with the crew chief. They then informed us that the problem was our own fault. We were the ones who brought the hippy invasion to White Lake and the problems that came with them were our doing. We should just live with it.

Mom, Pop, and I held an immediate executive meeting and decided that Yenta's was off-limits for the duration of the gangsters' stay. If we lay low, maybe they would, too. Besides, we reasoned, they were probably just selling drugs, which, in this case, was like selling ice in the Arctic. Still, until the eighteenth of August, when Bethel would return to its comatose state, and Yenta's to its former status—dead, empty, and very much for sale—we would stay away from the pancake house.

Besides, there were a lot of other things to worry about.

❧ ❧ ❧

The tickets for the concert were purchased by music stores, concert bureaus, shops, newsstands, and an endless stream of individual concertgoers. But as great as the ticket sales were, they didn't come close to reflecting the size of the crowd gathering at Yasgur's farm.

A medium-size city had begun to form on the grassy expanse of property that Max had set aside for the concert. Tens of thousands of people were now milling about, playing music, lying on blankets, and sleeping in tents and in their cars and vans. People of all colors and every ethnic, religious, and racial background had come together to create a huge quilt of humanity. Aerial photographs of the audience published in newspapers were at once awe-inspiring and terrifying. One could hardly believe the photographs for the sheer breadth and density of the population that had gathered.

The Woodstock crew had erected fences around the concert site in order to prevent the crowd from destroying all of Max's farmland. But the crowd was getting so big that it was clear that the fences wouldn't hold for long. By the fifth of August, everyone realized that the earlier projections of fifty thousand to seventy-five thousand people were ridiculously off the mark. Police estimated that when the concert opened on August fifteenth, at least two hundred thousand people would show up, and that the number might go as high as five hundred thousand.

For the most part, the crowd was peaceful, but there were skirmishes, arguments, and a few fights, all of which called into question the security measures that were in place. In fact, Woodstock

Ventures had created a security force that was designed to handle a much smaller number of people. If the crowd turned angry or violent, the only force capable of restoring order would be the National Guard. All of us began to realize that we were sitting on a dormant volcano which, if not handled properly, could destroy much of the region.

As the crowds got bigger and scarier, White Lake's antipathy for the Teichbergs became even more intense. Vandalism now became a daily occurrence. People drove by and threw garbage bags full of waste onto the property. At night, great quantities of horse manure were piled high in front of the newly named Faye Dunaway Wing and many of the bungalows. Rocks were thrown out of passing cars, and windows were routinely broken. Important equipment—our brand new lawn mower, for instance—was stolen. Vandals sneaked onto the property at night and poured red dye into the pool, turning the water the color of blood. The motel's exterior walls were regularly painted with curse words and threats. We were under siege.

All of these activities had a very strange effect on Pop. He actually got stronger and more animated as the Woodstock crowds got bigger and the locals more hostile. Combat with the hostile towns-folk brought the warrior out in him. It was some kind of weird tonic. Now he carried his baseball bat around the grounds with a pride that I had never seen before. Groups of young toughs appeared regularly on our property, issuing threats. Most of the encounters were just that—threats—but several involved physical attacks, as well.

One day, Pop prepared in advance for the day's onslaught by jumping in his little green pickup truck—its doors marked in white lettering, "White Lake Roofing Company"—and parking it in front of our office. The truck had a tar furnace on its bed. Pop fired up the furnace, heated the tar, and had it ready when a group of thugs approached the office. He put his mop into the tar and threatened to cover them in the hot substance if they came even a step closer to the office. He then stuck a flat stirrer into the tar and used it to fling tar balls at the group. You should have seen him laughing as he pelted them with wads of tar. What a great time he had chasing them off the property, firing tar at the backs of their heads.

This was a man who had spent his life bent over, slump shouldered, and defeated, not just by life's challenges, but by a wife who berated him daily. Now he was the king of the castle—a castle at full occupancy. He was making daily trips to the bank with bags of cash, and the motel was finally in the black. Now when cars full of hostile White Lakers drove by and taunted him, he gestured towards the cars parked in our lot or the "No Vacancy" sign outside the office. He wanted all of White Lake to know that we were doing great. Sometimes, when harassed from the street, he would just stand there and clap his baseball bat in his open palm, as if to say that he would enjoy taking them on if they were interested.

Pop saw more than his share of combat, too. One afternoon, a couple of men came walking onto our property and said that either we shut down the concert, or they would take off my head then and there. One of the thugs held a lead pipe, which he started whirling over his head in big circles. I told him to get off the property, but he started moving toward me. I looked around for a weapon, but nothing was available. Out of nowhere, Pop, clutching his baseball bat and looking very much like Mickey Mantle, came up from behind the guy with the pipe. Neither thug saw him. Pop swung low, like a good hitter going for a breaking ball. The bat's sweet spot found the backs of the guy's legs.

Thwack! The blow sent the thug to the ground in agony. The other thug suddenly turned to his partner in crime. But before he realized it, I lunged at him and landed a clean blow to his jaw. Both of them got to their feet and hurried off the property, one limping badly, the other holding the side of his face. Pop came over to me laughing, his eyes twinkling with glee. He put his arm around my shoulder and said, "You see, you see, we make them know they can't mess around with the Teichbergs." We both laughed out loud, relieved that we had survived the attack and very, very proud of ourselves.

Something strange and wonderful was happening between me and Pop. For the first time in our lives, we respected each other as men. Never before had we laughed together so much or hugged each other so much. We truly began to appreciate each other. But in this, we had help.

One of the great benefits of Woodstock—a benefit that, to my knowledge, has never been written about—was its sexual diversity. People of all sexual orientations were present at the concert in enormous numbers. And more important to me, many showed up at the El Monaco. One day, we had a sexual surrogate by the name of Victoria show up and hand me her card. She offered her services in exchange for a room. Momma ran her off the property before the two of us could negotiate. But even Momma couldn't stop the place from being filled with gays, lesbians, and people of ambiguous orientation.

And then, one day in early August, Georgette arrived.

She pulled up in a school bus that was painted in psychedelic colors. Flowers were artfully intertwined with serpents—the latter apparently in heat. The bus was a great work of DayGlo art, but the real work was Georgette herself. She opened the school bus doors and came down its stairs, all three hundred pounds of her, as if she were stepping onto a Broadway stage.

Wearing a June Allyson-type dress, with innocent ribbons in her shoulder-length hair, Georgette was a lesbian queen. She was originally from France, but had lived in the United States for the previous twenty years. Her voice, with its French accent, was soft, silky, and low, as if it were filtered through a Mister Softee ice cream machine before it left her mouth.

Georgette didn't come alone. She was accompanied by three larger-than-life women. Millie wore a frilly dress with daisies and ribbons tied in delicate bows. Hank and Yo-Yo, however, were tough trucker-types in overalls, plaid shirts, and construction boots.

Nor was Georgette's bus an ordinary one. As it turned out, it was a mobile Zen meditation and holistic healing center. In 1969, there weren't many American Buddhists driving around in their own psychedelic-meditation-healing temples, a fact that only added to the exotic appeal of this woman.

Apologetically, I told Georgette that we were booked solid, with not a square inch of floor space available. No problem, she told me. All she needed was a parking space for her bus.

The only physical space left was behind the barn theater, adjacent to the back wall, which, like the floor, was perilously slanted. I saw no reason why she couldn't park there for a month or so. In fact, the bus might help keep the wall up. Thus the temple on wheels procured a not-so-prime piece of White Lake real estate. This may have been the first lesbian Zen temple to ever appear in Sullivan County.

Once the four women set up camp on our property, the full blessing of their presence became apparent. First, they made no secret of their sexual preference. They even held little talks in the swamp on feminism, lesbianism, and the mythological roots of gay love. I was so overjoyed to have kindred spirits that I instantly refunded their rental fee and invited them to shoot out their tires and stay permanently.

Georgette and her friends modeled a degree of integration and peace with their sexuality that I had never seen before. Unlike the prototypical gay man, who is forced to screen other men before revealing his sexual orientation, Georgette broadcast her lesbianism with her every move. Within five minutes of meeting Georgette, people knew she was a homosexual—even those who were most in denial. Georgette, meanwhile, was nice to everyone. She wasn't angry; she didn't need to force-feed lesbianism to other people. On the contrary, she was completely relaxed about her orientation, which allowed others to be relaxed, too. For a gay man who had spent his entire life in the closet, she was a great teacher. But the fact that she was a woman made learning from her a little easier. Sometimes, I would be attracted to gay men who were comfortable with their sexuality, which complicated things instantly. But I could watch Georgette with eyes unobstructed by sexual yearning. She was a great mother figure, an earth goddess, a woman with magical powers who was as conversant in Buddhism and the healing arts as she was in the importance of being yourself.

Of course, all of these characteristics made Georgette a magnet for gay people at the El Monaco. People gathered around her in large part because they could freely be themselves. In fact, without any overt effort, her very presence demanded it. She was so honest, so open, and so relaxed, that she made you act the same way.

And maybe best of all, Georgette and her three friends made no secret of the fact that they loved me. These tough, courageous, honest women saw me as not only loveable, but inherently good. They didn't see me as Jewish, or fat, or ugly, or gay—all the things for which I had routinely been rejected over the years. They saw me as some kind of hero in this great, swirling, out-of-control miracle that was Woodstock.

One day, Georgette and I talked privately outside her bus. Ensconced in folding lawn chairs, we relaxed in the shade of a whispering pine tree.

"I have good news for you, Elliot," she told me.

"Oh, what is it?" I asked.

"Last night, the girls and I removed a curse from you."

"You did what?" I asked.

"We removed a curse from you, Elliot," she said. "The curse had blocked you from becoming yourself."

"I don't get it, Georgettte. What do you mean?"

"You were cursed by something in your past," Georgette said. "The curse caused you to hate yourself. I could see it in your aura field. There was black energy around the back of your head and down your spine. It was blocking you from receiving yourself, from embracing and receiving all that you really are. The girls and I got together last night and we removed it. Now the black energy is leaving you, and soon it will be gone entirely. It may take a little time, but you will become happier and happier now. Don't you feel lighter already?"

"Being around you always makes me feel better," I said. "But I guess I've always felt cursed. I even have a name for it. I call it the Teichberg Curse."

"Yes, you have had an intuitive knowledge of this thing, for sure. But now that the curse no longer has a hold on you, you will be able to realize your true spiritual potential."

"Well, that's good," I said. "But I'm an atheist, Georgette."

"In Buddhism, we say that there is no man upstairs who is God. We say that there is life and life goes on and on through infinity. We believe that life is a school and we keep coming back to learn lessons and to resolve our karma. Karma is just another word for cause-and-effect. If you make a good cause, you create good karma. If you make a mistake, or a bad cause, you create difficult karma. You have created many good causes, Elliot. Just look around you. Look at what you have helped create. It's all good karma, my friend. And it was time to get rid of that curse, no?"

"Yes," I said. I got up from my lawn chair and hugged her. Tears flowed down my face. What good cause had brought this goddess into my life? For the moment, it didn't matter what I believed about the Teichberg Curse, or whether I was free of it or not. She had seen me, even the darkest parts of me, and she loved me. That was healing enough.

After Georgette and I spoke that day, I began thinking more and more about coming out to my parents. I wanted to tell them that I was gay. I needed to tell them—and the world—who I really was. I just had to find the right moment.

Meanwhile, an odd thing began to unfold before my eyes. Pop and Georgette became great friends. In fact, the two were crazy about each other, and he clearly loved being around her. They began spending time together privately. I would be on my way over to the bus and find Georgette and Pop sitting together on her lawn chairs, talking away. What amazed me was that the two seemed to be having an intimate conversation. I often caught them laughing together. On other occasions, I would find Georgette talking quietly to Pop, and Pop would be nodding his head in agreement. What a strange sight—I had never seen Pop having an intimate talk with anyone in my entire life. But here he was with Georgette, making jokes and listening to her and nodding in agreement, as if they were sharing a deep truth. Whenever I noticed them chatting, I would sneak away without being seen.

Most amazing, when Georgette, Pop, and I were together, my father would communicate something to me through his look or, as Georgette would say, through his aura field. There was no mistaking it: Pop was sending me love. He softened and looked at me with pride. He had been doing that all summer—or rather, ever since Mike Lang and company showed up. But he was especially loving whenever the two of us were with Georgette. At first, I didn't recognize what was happening. Pop was getting old, after all. But then one day he smiled at me, and I realized that he knew I was gay and that he loved me and was proud of me.

I couldn't bear it. I went over to shack number two and had a long sit. Things were changing so fast, I could barely keep track of who I was becoming. The old me, whoever that might have been, was dissolving before my eyes. Who was this new me? I couldn't say exactly. I felt more settled, more sure, more at peace. Every aspect of my life had changed in the summer of '69. And now this—the look in my father's eyes when we made eye contact. Somewhere deep inside, I was still that little boy who patched roofs with his dad, all the time hoping he would see how hard I was working. And now, Woodstock, a great whirlwind of music and power, had swept into our town and changed us all.

Even Momma was changing. Of course, she was in heaven counting cash, depositing some of it, and hiding more in her secret places. She was so busy counting money that she didn't notice four entire Sabbaths come and go. To be fair, these were new experiences for us—depositing money rather than borrowing it or extending existing loans. Full occupancy was also a new experience, although the motel was at perhaps three times what could be legally called full occupancy.

Now, Momma's only problem was squaring her new prosperity with the Almighty. For this, she had to alter her nightly showdown with God. Normally, she would discuss her children's lives, my father's life, her various business ventures, and her own life—anything that she was trying to control at that moment in time. But now, with all this money flowing in, even on the Sabbath—a day when Jewish law forbids the handling of money—she had to make peace with the Almighty. I would hear her through the thin plywood walls that separated her bedroom from the office. No matter what was discussed, she usually ended her long nightly argument with God by making the same promises.

"God, I know you will excuse me for handling money on these few Sabbaths as this is mine desperate time of need. I know you wouldn't have sent this festival if you didn't want to help us, so I am working every day to show mine gratitude. Did Noah not work on the ark every day for forty days? As soon as this festival you sent us is over, I will make a nice donation and I'll make Elli go to shul, say Yizkor, get kosher, find a nice Jewish wife, and act normal! Thank you, God, for saving us from ruin."

Oy vey. Okay, so she still had a long way to go, especially when it came to recognizing her son as an adult who had his own life, a life that was no longer her responsibility to save. But I had learned to have realistic expectations of my mother a long time ago. And she was changing. Even I had to recognize it.

Maybe it was the money that was now in abundance, or the good vibes that radiated from the Woodstock crowd, or the clouds of hashish smoke floating through the compound each evening.

Maybe it was all of the above. Whatever the case, Momma was definitely becoming more human. She wasn't so shrill, and she wasn't so tight with money. I had never seen her so relaxed and, at times, genuinely generous with people—at least compared to what she had been before. She wasn't charging for every piece of soap or towel anymore. This was, for her, some weird form of charity. Truly, I marveled at this transformation. I only hoped it would live on after the festival was over.

But charity exists only when people believe they have more than enough for themselves. And the feeling of abundance was about to be threatened.

❈   ❈   ❈

At the beginning of August, we realized that we had a serious problem. We were quickly running out of food. I called wholesalers and requested literally dozens of trailers of bottled water, snack foods, soda, hot dogs, and other essentials. After the distributors stopped laughing and realized that I was serious, they requested payment in advance. I had no credit with suppliers. Moreover, I had no experience ordering food in such quantities, and didn't know if I was over- or under-ordering. Meanwhile, Mike was over his head with the demands of Woodstock. He was commuting to financial centers in New York to raise the funds needed to feed, protect, and provide sanitation for the enormous and unforeseen audience Woodstock Ventures now had on its hands. Pop and I talked it over and decided it would be wise to invest in two trailers of soda and two more trailers of food, and to request fifty more trailers on standby. As it turned out, the crowds became so enormous, and the food supply so short, we could have ordered fifty times that amount and still needed more.

The ever-growing city of hippies had the power to destroy all of Bethel—and all of Bethel knew it. Indeed, this knowledge terrified the townspeople to their bones. But the hippies also had the power to do something truly remarkable. None of us knew what would happen, and, if truth be told, we all were shaking in our boots.

11

The Day Is Saved

In the final ten days before the festival opened, space and time began to do strange and unpredictable things. Space contracted; the awareness of time was lost. Reality, at least the one shared by the residents of Bethel, had been co-opted by the counterculture. All the rules were different now.

Woodstock proved that when there is strength in numbers, people can exercise freedoms that are otherwise unavailable to them, especially if those freedoms harm no one. The young people who came to Woodstock smoked marijuana and took other drugs out in the open. They took off their clothes in public and swam naked in ponds and lakes. They walked over to the bushes and made love. Sometimes they didn't bother with the bushes. Men and women kissed; men and men kissed; women and women kissed. Lots of people got together and kissed all over the place. And they were doing all of this in numbers too great to comprehend.

Most of those who came to Woodstock remained at Yasgur's farm, but thousands more roamed Bethel and White Lake. People were everywhere, walking in droves along 17B on their way to Max's farm. They moved en masse on the streets and sidewalks of Bethel. No one could take a step without bumping into thousands of hippies; there was no place to go to shut out the life-altering event that was unfolding before our eyes. The world had come to Bethel, and the effect was both overpowering and disorienting.

Claustrophobia became an overwhelming problem. The locals were used to the quiet tranquility of open spaces and daily routines, which were the source of their security. Before Woodstock, grocery stores and shops around town were accustomed to one or two people entering at a time. Ten people in a shop at the same time was something akin to a riot. Now hundreds of people lined up to buy food, water, soda, toilet paper, and soap, and hundreds more were on the way.

Of course, prices went through the roof. Water was being sold for five dollars a bottle. Loaves of bread, packages of luncheon meats, bottles of soda, and cartons of milk were becoming increasingly precious. Food began to run out, which only added to the fear and, for some, the hysteria.

One group—the Hog Farm, a commune organized in the early '60s—actually provided free food. Apparently, Mike Lang and his partners had asked the commune's organizer, a man named Wavy Gravy, to help with security at the festival. Gravy agreed, and also set up a kitchen to supply festival goers with food. Later on, the farm would boast that it had provided "breakfast in bed for 400,000 people." No doubt, this food helped keep the peace.

At the El Monaco, we witnessed firsthand the dangers that food shortages could bring. That week, the two truckloads of food that Pop and I had ordered finally arrived at the motel. No sooner had we unloaded the food than word of the delivery spread at the concert site. Within hours, a mob consisting of a few hundred people arrived and raced toward the trucks, ready to tear off the doors and take whatever they could find. Pop hurried to the trucks, flung open the rear doors, and showed the crowd that both vehicles were empty. You could feel disappointment and anger rippling through the crowd. Neither Pop nor I knew what the mob might do next, but visions of them storming the motel and tearing down everything until food was found came to mind.

Suddenly, a young man with a guitar climbed onto the roof of one of the trucks, sat down, and began singing Bob Dylan's classic "Blowin' in the Wind." And thank God, the kid could sing. His voice rang out strong and clear.

The crowd looked up at the boy with a mixture of surprise and awe. And then something came over everyone—their anger melted away. You could see their shoulders relax and their bodies loosen. Many smiled and laughed. Others joined in the singing. In less than two minutes, the rage was gone. Some put their arms around each other. Others walked away quietly, and in no time, the crowd had dispersed peacefully. Music's gentle power would not be denied.

Fortunately, the food problems did not become dire. The Woodstock partners arranged to have supplies of food, water, and other essentials flown into town by helicopter—the only quick way to get into White Lake. The cars and trucks on Route 17B were moving at a crawl, when they moved at all.

Every square foot of our property at the El Monaco was rented. We even rented out the swamp, where people camped out in cars, school buses, and vans. Multiple groups were packed into rooms, as well as odd spaces that Pop and I had turned into rooms. More than five hundred people were residing at the El Monaco now, and even I didn't know where we kept all of them.

Pop and I filled the pool with drinking water and then set up hoses throughout the compound so that people could come in and get free water when they needed it. It was a miracle that our four spring water wells and their respective pumps kept working despite daily threats by the locals, who promised to poison the water or destroy the pumps. We opened the pool shower to anyone who wanted to bathe. Soap, like so many other basics, was long gone.

Out of necessity, we turned the El Monaco into a makeshift first aid center for hundreds of people who showed up with cuts and bruises, or in need of a safe place to come down from a bad drug trip. I got every blanket I could find in the motel inventory and rushed to wrap shivering bodies that were coming down off a bender. Pop and I dug trenches in the crawl spaces under the motel buildings and created emergency "beds." People, most of them young, turned up out of nowhere to help us deal with those who were stoned or injured in an accident. We had an ongoing triage center, but if Pop and I couldn't get to someone who needed help, three or four people would appear to take care of anyone who had to be patched up.

Frantic family members from all over the world called us daily to ask if we had seen loved ones, shutting down phone lines for extended periods of time. Our lives had been taken over by what had to be done at that moment. We surrendered to the demands of this new reality, which forced us to care for others and do whatever we could to help those in need. Woodstock was a life force unto itself, with its own code, and powerful beyond our wildest dreams. Everyone in Bethel knew that they had lost control of events. Many were willing to ride the wave, but most were just plain terrified.

Of course, the big fear among the townies was that the hippies would riot and flatten Bethel. Rumors swirled that unspeakable atrocities were being committed at Yasgur's farm. Hells Angels were on the loose, some were saying, stealing people's money and committing rape and murder. Hippies were having group sex. Everyone was stoned and going crazy. Dogs and cats were humping each other. None of it was true—well, at least the rumors of violence weren't true. But the rumors were enough to ignite terror in the locals and send them over the edge.

It was clear to me that if things got ugly, we'd need more security at the El Monaco. All we had was Pop, his baseball bat, and me. Momma, despite her good work against the Mafia, could not be counted on in a riot. The best she could do was put an old Russian curse on people, but its effects would take time. We needed a soldier or two. Unfortunately, there was no one on whom we could count—that is, until Vilma showed up.

Early that August, I left my office in the middle of a rainstorm. Right before me, standing in the soggy mud and grass, was a tall, stout woman holding a large black umbrella and staring at me. She was at least six feet two, wearing a black sequined dress, fishnet stockings, and spike heels. Her makeup was so thick you could have used it for wallpaper paste. Her false eyelashes were like two pairs of black teeth. Her faux hair was piled high, fastened with lacquered chopsticks, and so stiff with spray that it could have given Brillo a run for its money.

I hadn't seen her check in—trust me, I would have remembered. I stared back at her, watching as her spike heels sank into the mud. She reminded me of Marlene Dietrich, with an extra hit of testosterone and a lot more miles under her belt. Still, she was a vision, I must admit. Her gaze didn't waver. Indeed, it seemed to beckon me.

"Permit me to introduce myself," she said. "I don't believe we've met." What was that accent—Russian, German, Jersey? Some mixture of all three, I decided. "I am Baroness Von Vilma. I have been watching you for a few days. You don't look like a golf-cart type of man. What are you doing?"

"I am the owner," I told her.

"Ah, a man of property. I knew you were more than a caddie and less than a cad. I am here to offer you my services. You look like a man who could appreciate me."

As she said this, she pulled from the handle of her umbrella an impressive leather cat-o'-nine-tails. I didn't know how to react. I had never been involved with a dominatrix before.

"Maybe you have a brother in leather?" I said with a smile.

"I can be most accommodating," the Baroness said. And with that, she parted her sequined dress and showed me her secret. *She was a guy!*

Vilma was probably the first transvestite ever to set foot in White Lake. I don't shock easily—I've pretty much seen it all when it comes to sex—but I must admit that Vilma caught me off guard. While I didn't fully understand my reaction, I clearly needed to decline her offer. Perhaps on another occasion I might have felt different, but these days, I was in some kind of weird transition. Sex between the two of us was not meant to be, I explained.

Vilma was disappointed, but she understood. She sighed and then said, "Well, maybe you would like for us to have a cold drink. Would that be more to your liking?" she asked.

"That would be fine," I told her.

We went to Vilma's room, where she had a cold bottle of Coca-Cola and a couple of paper cups, which she filled for both of us. As we drank our Coke, Vilma told me something of her background. She was, in fact, a sergeant under General George Patton during the Second World War. She even showed me an array of photos to prove it. Of course, she looked considerably different in her military uniform, but there was no mistaking her. Now she was a grandfather eight times over, and a transvestite and occasional hooker, as well.

"You're an inspiration," I said. And then inspiration hit me.

"Vilma, I need the help of some, uh, strong people around here," I told her. "The locals are angry at me for bringing Woodstock to Bethel, and they occasionally show up looking for trouble. So far, my Pop and I have been able to fend them off, but things could get a little dicey from here on. Could you help us patrol the grounds—you know, act as security—when you're not busy doing other things?"

"It would be an honor, Elliot," she told me.

The two of us shook hands and Vilma nearly crushed mine, which seemed to confirm the wisdom of my decision.

As luck would have it, a couple of young thugs were painting a swastika on the side of the Faye Dunaway Wing when Vilma and I walked out of her room. We hurried over to stop them, but before we got there, a group of hippies descended on the punks. "What are you doing?" one of the hippies screamed. "What's all this hate?" One of the hippies ripped the paintbrush out of the artist's hand. Some pushing followed, and the next thing I knew, the hippies were wrestling the two thugs to the ground. Pop ran onto the scene, baseball bat in hand, and supervised the thrashing. Then he got the pile of hippies off the vandals. "You get out of here," he told them. "Otherwise, I stick this bat in your eye."

I turned to Vilma and said, "See what I mean? We need help."

"Elliot, I will keep my eyes peeled and my whips handy."

"Thank you, Vilma. I feel better already."

✳ ✳ ✳

Monday, August eleventh, began as a beautiful summer day, with a clear sky, low humidity, and a glistening, nourishing energy in the air. *What could disturb such a morning?* I thought. And then I got my answer. Five members of the Bethel Town Council and two or three more local businessmen marched onto our property and headed for the door of my tiny office. They all had their game faces on—pissed off and resolute, an attitude that intensified as they approached the office.

Partly blocking our front door were eight or nine young men and women, all of them wrapped in blankets and sleeping bags, sound asleep. The council members stepped over, around, and between the hippies, eyeing them with loathing. The chore of getting through the sleeping bodies seemed to annoy the town fathers all the more. One look at their ruddy complexions told me that this was not going to be a pleasant little chat.

After they had elbowed and shouldered their way into our tiny office, their leader, a middle-aged man with a considerable gut and a bald head, made an announcement.

"The community of White Lake has had enough," he began. "We do not want this festival. The town council has declared that the town of Bethel is in a state of emergency. We have petitioned Governor Rockefeller and asked him to ratify our declaration, and send in the National Guard to clear the area of all the hippies and misfits who are destroying our community. We will not tolerate any further damage. If you and your trash don't vacate this county immediately, we will block Route 17B with a human barrier on Friday morning! No one will get through to Yasgur's farm! This is the only warning we're going to give you. We represent the business community of White Lake, the merchants, the homeowners, and even Yasgur's neighbors. Do you understand what I am saying, Elliot?"

"What's the matter?" I asked them. "Didn't you get enough money? Do you want more, is that what you want?"

"What money are you talking about?" one of the businessmen asked.

A member of the town council broke in with a warning. "Be careful what you say! You never saw any money pass hands."

"There's a lot of money in this thing and you all know it," I said. "What are you really looking for—more money? Or are you just trying to get reelected?"

"It was one thing when you said twenty or thirty thousand people were coming here," the leader resumed. "This is not what you said would happen. This is half a million people. Just look down 17B! You Jews are making big bucks here. You pulled a fast one on us and you're not going to get away with it! If you think your festival is going to happen, you're dreaming! We're not letting more hippies onto 17B."

Pop—carrying his baseball bat—stepped into the office, and right behind him was Vilma, all six feet two inches of her. Suddenly, Vilma's voice boomed. "What is going on here, I want to know!" With that, she snapped her whip hard against the door. The Chihuahuas looked first at Vilma and then at Pop, his bat at the ready, and froze.

"You're trespassing on private property," I yelled. "Get the hell out of here. Now!" Right on cue, Vilma snapped her whip again.

It was as if someone had yelled "Bomb!" Pop and Vilma could barely get out of way fast enough to accommodate the mad dash of the Chihuahuas out of my office.

The next thing I did was find Mike Lang, my white knight in ringlets, who was sitting on his motorcycle, ready to leave for Yasgur's. I explained the latest developments.

"No problem, man," Mike said. He then got off the bike, went into his office, and made a telephone call to one of his partners. After hanging up, he said, "No problem, Elliot. We're on top of this barrier shit."

Lang escorted me out of his office and asked me to wait there for a few minutes. He then went over to the rooms occupied by the networks—ABC, CBS, and NBC. A few minutes later, he exited one of the network offices and walked over to me.

"Elli, how about you going on NBC radio in about an hour?" Mike asked. "Room 102. Tell the whole country to come up to the festival now. Tell them not to wait. Tell them what's going down. Tell them about those rotten politicos, man. Tell them about the barricade. Tell them the festival is alive and well and happening. Tell them it's the birth of a new nation, the Woodstock Nation. Use your own words, just make sure that they know to come up now. Okay, Elli?"

I realized instantly what Mike was getting at. He knew that the more people who came to the festival, the less power the town council—or even the governor—would have to stop it.

"Okay," I said.

Together, we walked over to Room 102, which felt to me like a mile from where I had been standing. In fact, the networks had been at the El Monaco for the past couple of weeks, having arrived right after I gave my press conference. NBC had occupied Room 102, which was one of the ten rooms we first built after expanding beyond the rooming house. Before the appearance of the news people, the room had been furnished with cheap castoffs of my three sisters, and painted in pastels purchased at garage sales. The NBC execs took one look at the place and threw out all the furniture. They then painted the walls black and installed enormous banks of radio and television equipment, microphones, cables, monitors, and lots of telephones.

I knocked on the door and Mike and I were let in. I felt as if I were walking into another world. Both sides of the room were lined with electronic equipment, where half a dozen technicians with headsets and microphones pushed buttons and adjusted knobs. The director called me over to a table upon which sat a microphone. "Have a seat here in front of the mike, Elliot," he told me. Another tech put a headset on me. Mike Lang took a position in the back of the room.

Realizing that I was about to address millions of people, I trembled inside. For a moment, I felt my legs go limp. Could I do this? My entire life had led me here. I felt both my own dream and the dream of the festival weighing on me. The very life of Woodstock, and all that it meant to people, was on the line.

In minutes, the program began, and one of the men announced that we were live from Woodstock. "With us is Elliot Tiber, owner of the El Monaco Motel, where we and many of the Woodstock staff are staying. Elliot, what do you have to tell us?"

Somewhere in my brain, two things happened. First, I went fuzzy and everything seemed to blur. Then, I somehow caught a wave and a gust of energy blew through me, lacing my tongue with words—words that tumbled out of my mouth with a power that I hadn't possessed seconds before.

I told the country that the Woodstock Music and Arts Festival would start, as expected, on the fifteenth of August—just four days from now! I invited one and all to come up to Bethel immediately. Don't wait, I told them. Come now so that you're sure to get a spot at Yasgur's farm.

Then I explained that the Bethel Town Council was trying to put a stop to the festival. But I further explained that this was not going to happen.

"They cannot stop us legally," I said. "We have all the legal permits and we're going forward with the concert. Instead, they plan to block traffic with a human barricade to keep people from entering Bethel. We need you to come up here and support this festival. If people try to stop your car when you arrive, just drive around them, or park your car and walk around them. Just walk right into Bethel to Yasgur's farm. We're waiting for you, and the promoters have decided that anyone who comes to the Woodstock festival now can come to the concert for free.

"This is more than a music and arts festival. This is the birth of a new nation—the Woodstock Nation. We're against the war. We honor freedom, music, and civil rights for all people. Come up here and be a part of Woodstock Nation!" I finished by giving driving directions from New York City to White Lake.

The glorious wind that had filled my sails now left me just as abruptly. I rose from my chair feeling exhausted, as if I'd just been in a fight.

I had no idea if anyone out there in radio land had heard what I said. There was no feedback, no conversation with listeners—just me talking into a metal mesh-covered object and hoping that people throughout the country would hear me and start making their way toward Bethel.

The technical crew members gave me the okay sign and Mike gave me a transcendent smile. "You cooked, man. Right on. That was beautiful."

That evening, Route 17B was quiet. Yes, the traffic continued to flow into Bethel, but the number of cars had dwindled. Now I was sure that no one had heard me.

Later that night, the El Monaco dance bar was packed with people listening to a jam session given by a couple from Bombay. The couple was playing mysterious stringed instruments that I assumed were sitars. The night was quiet and the mood was mellow. Miserably, I noted that the traffic entering Bethel had reduced to a mere trickle.

At the back of the bar was a door that opened on to a spare bedroom, where I often crashed for a few hours or an entire night. Now I opened the door and, fully clothed, fell onto a mattress. I was asleep almost instantly. I don't know how long I slept, but I was suddenly awakened by the sound of car horns blaring. Immediately, I thought that local goons were attacking us. I got out of bed, wobbly with exhaustion, and grabbed a hammer. Then I opened the door to the bar and found Pop, fully clothed and asleep on one of the mattresses that lay in a corner of the room. Next to him was Momma, also asleep in her clothes. I nudged Pop awake. Hearing the car horns, he jumped up, grabbed his baseball bat, and stood by my side. Then Momma awakened and, seeing the bat in Pop's hand and the hammer in mine, looked around for an appropriate weapon. On a shelf near the bar was an empty bottle of King David kosher wine. She grabbed the bottle and joined Pop and me as we approached the door.

Pop, Momma, and I opened the bar doors and walked out into the night, expecting to meet our fate before a horde of rabid townies. Instead, we saw a miracle. There, like a beautiful necklace of sparkling diamonds, was a double chain of shining headlights entering Bethel. From the high ground where we were standing, we could look south and see the lights moving toward us for miles along 17B. This was no Armageddon. This was Moses leading the people to Bethel—which in Hebrew means *House of God.*

Pop, his bat down at his side; Momma, with her kosher wine bottle; and I, still holding my hammer, stood there, bathed in a river of light. We watched the cars and trucks come into town, people occasionally calling out to us. "Hey, El Monaco, we heard you on the radio!" more than one said. "We got your message!" others called out. The cars and trucks, many painted in DayGlo colors, were filled with the young, the old, and every age in between. They carried people of every color—black, white, yellow, brown, and red. Many flashed the peace sign; others waved. And at three o'clock in the morning, everyone was happy and more than ready to party.

Elation ran through me like healing waters.

"I don't believe these people are here for our swingin' singles weekend, Pop. What do you think?" He just smiled and waved back to the people who waved at us. I had never felt so much love—and redemption—in my entire life.

Finally, the three of us went to our rooms and fell asleep.

In the morning, we turned on our single working television set and saw news footage of the New York State Thruway, which was jammed from New York City to the Bethel exit. Other footage revealed that alternate highways and side roads to Bethel were completely packed, as well. Finally, the reporter showed Route

17B, the cars stopped dead for miles. "Welcome to the world's largest parking lot," he said.

I was in heaven. Pop looked at me, his dark eyes flashing with light. It was enough to break and heal my heart all at once.

I jumped out of my chair and said, "This calls for a new sign." I got my brushes, paints, and a wide piece of plywood and wrote:

Welcome to the Woodstock Festival.
Welcome Home.

I hung the sign right out in front of our dance bar, directly over the old sign that said, "Motel for Sale—At a Price You Can Afford."

Later that morning, the police turned 17B into a five-lane highway, with all five lanes going in the same direction. When I looked out at the packed stretch of road, I said to myself, *Let them try to stop us now.*

✳   ✳   ✳

The following day—Tuesday, the twelfth of August—Mike Lang and the entire entourage of Woodstock staffers left the El Monaco and moved to Yasgur's farm. The El Monaco was empty for all of three hours—the time it took us to fill every room and alternative space in the entire compound. In a single day, we went from being overbooked, to empty, to overbooked again.

The next day, Wednesday, I was trying to catch up on paperwork when a stranger stepped into my office. At first, I thought he was just another gangster from central casting looking for his associates in Yenta's Pancake House. He wore a dark three-piece suit and pointed shoes made from some dead reptile—this in the middle of hippieville, where even jeans and sandals were optional.

"You're probably looking for your associates over at Yenta's," I told him. "Just walk in that direction and you're sure to bump into them."

"I'm looking for you, Tiber," he said with menacing gravity.

"What can I do for you?"

"You're going to shut down this festival now, or we're going to shut you down—permanently—when the thing is over."

I had grown used to threats of all kinds, and most didn't mean a thing to me anymore, but this guy gave me a jolt. His manner was threatening and I was a little unhinged by the very real sense of danger that surrounded him.

"I don't have any control over this festival," I said. "We all lost control of this thing about a month ago."

"Let me put this in perspective for you. You're gonna close this thing down now, or you're gonna go out with a real big bang. Enjoy the next few days, Tiber. Have a good long look at your El Monaco, because there are people—big people—who say you ain't gonna have no motel once these creeps and drug-crazed hippies of yours are outta here. We're done with all the legal crap, you understand me? I don't think too much of you or your kind. And it will be a pleasure to put you and this place down."

With that, he opened the button of his jacket. I could see the glimmer of a metal object beneath his coat.

Before I could say "Mike Lang, help!" the Baroness Von Vilma stepped into the office, having just completed her security round of the El Monaco compound. Today, she was dressed in a woman's military uniform—one that was a bit too tight for her, I might add. Her padded breasts strained the brass buttons of her jacket. Meanwhile, her five o'clock shadow, already in full bloom at noon, was showing through her thick coat of makeup. Yes, to my rescue came an unshaven, extraordinarily decorated military man, dressed in a woman's army uniform. What could be more appropriate?

"Elliot!" the Baroness called out in her deep bass voice. "Is this man bothering you?"

Quickly, I explained the situation.

In an instant, Vilma whipped out a small silver pistol that, for all I could tell, was a fancy cap gun. Whatever it was, it looked real enough to all concerned. And Vilma was deadly serious. Suddenly, she dropped the accent and let her real voice be heard.

"You want to get out of here fast, pal, or I'm going to put a couple of holes in that fancy suit of yours. And if I see you here again, I'm going to shoot you on sight. Capisce?"

I don't know what scared the gangster more—Vilma's gun or Vilma herself. The guy threw up his hands, raised his eyebrows into his hairline, and hurried out the door.

⊕　　⊕　　⊕

The nonstop activity was starting to get to me. I was exhausted, but I knew I couldn't rest. I had to stay on top of things as best I could, because so much was at stake—both personally and for the event that was changing my life. Still, I could see that my parents' energy was flagging. They were old and the hard work and daily assaults were taking a toll on them. They needed a break, I decided. They needed to calm down and take a mini-vacation.

So I cooked up a batch of hash cookies. People were storing enormous quantities of hashish and marijuana in the freezer of our bar, and I procured a quantity—just enough to mellow everyone out. Then I folded the hash into the cookie dough, added chocolate chips, and baked for twelve minutes. Voilà! Happy cookies! Actually, I'd heard of hash brownies before, but I hadn't come across hash cookies. I was curious about what effect, if any, the cookies would have.

With the cookies baked and cooled, I told my parents to come over to the bar for some refreshments. These days, the bar was functioning more as a shelter from the periodic bursts of rain and as a pit stop for passersby—we offered water and one of the few working public toilets. Mom and Dad found an empty table and I served us all a big batch of cookies and coffee. They both wolfed down the cookies and drank the coffee. Then they passed the cookies around to others in the bar. "Oh Eliyahu, these are good cookies. They are kosher, right, Eliyahu? You don't want your poor mother to be making God unhappy now."

"I'm sure that these cookies would make any rabbi very happy, Momma," I told her.

At first, I didn't think either of them could get stoned—they were both so serious, hard-working, worried, and flat-out terrified most of the time. Nevertheless, in a little while I could see the hash doing its magic. Pop was the first to have a reaction. He just started laughing and giggling at nothing in particular. His whole body convulsed with laughter. "You see those kids who was painting our walls, they looked so funny when I got all of those hippies off them, like they was going to pee in their pants. Did you see that, Eliyahu? Did you see that?"

"Yeah, Pop, I saw it." Pop just kept laughing and giggling.

The next thing I knew, Momma was laughing, too. She was laughing so hard that I suddenly feared she might break a rib.

"What's so funny, Mom?" I asked her.

"Look at this place," she said through her laughter. "It's such a mess. People everywhere. People here, people in the rooms, people under the building, people on the roof, people in the swamp, people on top of the trucks and cars and vans. We got people coming out of our ears."

When the two of them stopped laughing, they just sat there, content with the world. I had really never seen them so relaxed. I dragged a mattress over to our table and the next thing I knew, my two worn-out and stoned parents slumped in their chairs, asleep. I rolled them onto the waiting bed. And then I got myself a mattress and collapsed for about three hours of R and R.

❧ ❧ ❧

When Mike Lang and company left the El Monaco for Yasgur's farm, I felt the loss. Yes, we were fully booked in a matter of hours, but the money wasn't what was motivating me anymore. I loved the adventure, and Mike brought that in spades. When he showed up, all of Bethel came alive. I did, too. My life had never been so challenging—or threatening—as it was after Mike Lang came to town. This was the most fun I had ever had in my life, and I knew that I was different for the experience, though I couldn't yet say exactly how. And now Mike and his crew were over at Max's. The festival would take place—he would see to that—and in a few days, the Woodstock Ventures team would be gone. So would all my gay, lesbian, and straight friends. White Lake would go back to being bored and boring. Maybe a hit man or two would come after me, but that wouldn't be as much fun as it was when Mike and Vilma and Georgette were there.

So I did the only thing that came to mind—I found a way to get over to Max's farm to see what the center of the universe looked like. Driving over in the car was out of the question now. I need-ed a motorcycle, but Mike's Harley was with him at the site. I'd have to hitch a ride on someone's bike, and for that, I'd have to get lucky. I walked out to Route 17B and there, sitting on a bike in traffic, was a New York State Trooper. He was wearing mirrored sunglasses, a white motorcycle helmet, and a blue state trooper's uniform. He was about my height, as far as I could make out, and in good shape, strong and lean. It was just intuition, but he seemed like a good guy, not one of those mean cops who sees everyone as a rapist or murderer. I decided to take a chance.

"Hi, I'm Elliot Tiber, the guy who helped start this whole mess," I told the trooper. "I own this motel."

The trooper nodded at me and gave me a sly smile, well aware that half the residents of White Lake would love it if he drew his gun and shot me then and there. His expression encouraged me to keep talking.

"You know," I said, "even though I had a hand in this thing—and mind you, mine was only one of many hands—I haven't been over to the farm in a couple of weeks and I would love to see what it looks like now that the concert's about to begin. Do you think you could give me a ride to Yasgur's?"

"Yeah, sure," the trooper said. "Hop on." Once I got on the back, the trooper insisted that I put my arms around his waist. "If you fall off, it's my ass that gets busted," he explained.

"Gotcha," I said. Now it was my turn to give a sly smile.

Darting between lanes of traffic, we arrived at Max's farm in less than fifteen minutes. I stood at the edge of Yasgur's in utter amazement. I had visited this farm on a regular basis for the previous fourteen years, and now it was unrecognizable to me.

In less than a month, Mike Lang, John Roberts, Joel Rosenman, and Artie Kornfeld—along with a few hundred Woodstock staffers—had created a mini-city the likes of which I could not have dreamed possible. The landscape itself was an enormous bowl, a perfect amphitheater. At the south end of the theater stood the stage, which had to be a hundred feet wide. Over the stage were long canvas covers that would protect the equipment and the performers from the weather. To either side of the stage were enormous speakers, amplifiers, and other electronic equipment. At the center of the stage stood a quintet of microphones awaiting their masters—Havens; Joplin; Daltrey; Hendrix; Baez; Guthrie; Sly; Creedence; Cocker; Country Joe; Crosby, Stills, Nash, and Young, and many many more. The scaffolding that supported the stage stood three stories high. Behind the stage and to its left and right were hordes of tents, along with dozens of trailers, trucks, buses, and tractors. Miles and miles of cable and wire ran from the stage to the sound equipment. Booms and cranes reached out like long robotic arms high above the huge platform.

A few hundred yards in front of the stage stood another array of scaffolds—all of them three stories high—holding more speakers. Throughout the grounds were hundreds of tents, some of them tiny pup tents, others larger and more elaborate, and all in different colors, from yellow to blue to red. Concession stands, built of poles and covered with tan canvas, stood like friendly sentinels around the grounds. At the edges of the grounds were scattered battalions of cars, pickup trucks, and buses painted in bright psychedelic patterns. And spread across the entire field were five hundred thousand people, all of them bound together like multicolored threads in a vast and elaborate carpet. It was breathtaking, inspiring, and dizzying all at once. I scanned the crowd and saw the gentle joy written on everyone's face. This is what Mike Lang was seeing out here—the generation that opposed war and gave rise to the civil rights movement. These were the faces that had inspired him to name this generation Woodstock Nation.

Throughout the sea of smiling faces, people were playing guitar and singing. Choruses of voices arose from every direction in every language imaginable. Those who didn't play guitar had fashioned crude musical instruments out of recycled metal, wood, and fabric. Folks were hawking all sorts of chachkas, souvenirs, newspapers, political and social petitions, and drug and sex paraphernalia. There was an endless variety of groups as well—Hare Krishnas, Vietnam veterans, vets against the war, antiwar protesters, black militants, people advocating the legalization of drugs, and those who wanted to ban all drugs. There were Christians, Jews, Muslims, Hindus, and sects of all kinds, all cohabiting on blankets and in tents, all with the same intention: To enjoy and be uplifted by the music and its vision.

You couldn't get within three hundred yards of the stage—the population was too dense for anyone to move freely there—so I stayed along the periphery and continued my tour. As I walked along, taking in the scene around me, I happened upon a parked van that had brilliant flowers painted all over its exterior. The sliding doors were open, and lanterns illuminated the interior, which was lined with colorful rugs. The sweet smell of incense wafted from within, along with some rock 'n' roll music. A slender girl of about twenty-five years of age, with long brown hair, big brown eyes, and a sweet smile, swayed gently to a beat that was very different from the music that emanated from the van's stereo. Lying inside the van, stretched out on a large beanbag cushion, was her companion—a young man with long blonde hair, a swimmer's body, and a vacant smile on his face. All he had on was a pair of khaki shorts.

The two looked at me and the young man said, "Hey man, come on in, join us." I poked my head in the van. The young man held up a tiny bit of paper with a dot on it. "Just put it on your tongue, man. It's a trip."

"What is it?"

"No idea, babe. But it sure is good times all packed into one itsy-bitsy dot. Oh yeah. They call it instant travel package. I'm feeling no pain."

The woman ran her hands on my neck while I licked the paper. Both the man and the woman helped me get into the van and lie down on the beanbag pillow, next to the man. Then the woman lay down next to me on my other side. At first I didn't feel anything. I didn't even feel the micro-dot dissolve. I was too focused on the emerald eyes of the young swimmer. Something within urged me to lie back and let go of all my suffocating responsibilities—the motel, my parents, the endless battles, the people who hated me, and those who thought I was a hero. *Just let it all go,* the voice inside me said. And in a single moment, I dissolved into the music while the girl's silky hands did a sexual dance all over my body.

"In a few minutes you'll get a real nice buzz," she said. "Relax. Don't worry. We'll be with you the whole time."

Now the young man started to run his hands along my legs and the two of them reached inside my pants. At that point, I was gone. For the next span of time—what was it, ten minutes, ten hours, or ten days?—I was in a state of bliss, unlike any bliss I'd ever experienced, read about, or fantasized. Shapes and colors and moods passed through me with the silkiness of honey. The shapes spoke the most beautiful words to me. I conversed with beautiful colors. To this day, I have no idea what the shapes and colors said to me. I only know that it was as sweet as love.

Meanwhile, sexual fantasies flickered through my mind and then each one was fulfilled. My two travel companions and I starred in a film of sexual delights. As one sexual event after another unfolded, the faces and bodies of my companions kept transforming. Sometimes they were beautiful physical bodies and sometimes just shadows, their eyes little more than flickering lights. There were moments when I entered their bodies. I don't know how, but I was inside of both of them, often at the same time. And then I was plummeting into a black hole in space. I became small and then spun recklessly outward. Sensations of joy and wonder turned into unrelenting terror that eventually became peace and stillness. Colors gyrated and danced. I felt as if space were moving through me, rather than me moving through space. Meanwhile, I was caressed by the two tender people with whom I traveled. It was terrifying and wonderful at the same time.

The journey lasted several hours, I assume. But finally I found myself being talked down by the couple. They taught me to concentrate on my breathing and to say certain incantations that would protect me as the drug wore off. Finally, the couple told me about the incredible three-way sexual experience we had just shared. They called it a mutual sexual journey. They then taught me a few more incantations that they promised would protect and guide me in the future.

Most of what I could remember about the sex was the gentle touching and expressions of love that the two lavished on me. Wild frenzy was all I had ever known of sex. This kind of lovemaking—and that is the only word that really fits the experience—was unlike anything I had ever known.

And that was my first experience with LSD.

I was still moving through a dense haze when I started to regain my senses, but somehow people got me back to the El Monaco, where the high-speed insanity hadn't missed a single beat. Mom and Pop were taking calls, handling the usual stampede of demands and complaints. I managed to pitch in—maybe I changed some bedding, or took a registration or two—but I don't recall a single detail of what I did. Later that afternoon, I fell into bed and slept until the following morning.

❧ ❧ ❧

It rained that Friday, the day the festival began, but the weather didn't stop people from coming to Woodstock. The traffic, which had peaked the previous Monday night, remained high. As the television news reporter said, 17B was reduced to a parking lot. So concertgoers simply abandoned their cars and walked to Yasgur's farm, thus turning much of 17B into a sidewalk.

True to their word, about a dozen members of the Bethel Town Council and assorted hangers-on showed up with their wives to form a human barricade against the tens of thousands of people traveling to the festival. It was, in all respects, a most pathetic and ineffective effort.

The men forming the blockade were dressed in plaid pants and candy colored shirts, the women in shirtwaist dresses. They carried little signs, written on white paper plates, that said, "Festival Canceled by Order of the Town Board of White Lake. Vacate White Lake Immediately." The hippies, young and old, just walked around and through the barricade, completely unfazed by the town council's demands. As far as the hippies were concerned, the council members were speaking gibberish.

In a most unexpected way, the barricade was proof that the generation which had accepted racism and sexual discrimination as a matter of course—that had given us the atomic bomb and the

Vietnam War—was simply too used to accepting the status quo to launch an effective protest against anything. I might have laughed at them were it not for the fact that I found their efforts so terribly sad—and, yes, even pitiful. With all the horrors taking place in the world, they had channeled their energy into stopping three days of music, peace, and love.

12

Taking Woodstock

On Friday, August 15, 1969, at five o'clock in the afternoon, Richie Havens officially opened the Woodstock Music and Arts Festival with a set of nine songs. Havens was not scheduled to go on first, but he was the only act available at the time. The roads were choked with traffic in every direction, rendering them impassable. The only way to get the performers to White Lake was to helicopter them in. Mike Lang begged Havens to take the stage, and he reluctantly agreed.

As it turned out, there could not have been a more perfect opening to the concert. Determined yet humble, like someone who views his mission as more important than himself, Richie Havens walked on stage, his guitar under his arm, and spoke to a sea of expectant faces. "People are going to read about you tomorrow and how really groovy you were," he told the crowd. "All over the world, if you can dig where that's at." And then he started playing his guitar fast and furious, like a man possessed.

The huge speakers at Max's farm sent Havens' pounding guitar music bouncing off the hills and valleys of White Lake for all to hear. The singer's gravelly voice—so honest in its longing—captured the heart and soul of a country crying out for an end to war and the spread of equality among all people. There were few people alive who could have better expressed the spirit of the times, and the pain at the center of the human heart.

Despite the many weeks of threats from locals and the town's shortsighted resistance, the Woodstock festival had actually begun. And now the powerful musical voices of a new generation were taking center stage.

That night, Arlo Guthrie stood on the stage and reported the latest police estimates of the size of the crowd. "I don't know how many of you can dig how many people there are, man," Arlo intoned in his characteristic nasal twang. "I was rapping to the fuzz, right? Can you dig it? Man, there's supposed to be a million and a half people here by tonight. Can you dig that? The New York State Thruway is closed, man."

Later on, state and local officials would put the number at Yasgur's farm at five hundred thousand. They said a million more was on the way but stuck in traffic, which was backed up to the George Washington Bridge, some ninety miles away. But I believe those estimates were conservative in the extreme. This was far bigger than any New Year's Eve at Times Square, which routinely claimed up to a million people.

Contrary to all the fears and rumors that circulated before the concert began, there was virtually no crime or violence at the festival. There were no riots, no rapes, no attacks on the locals. In fact, when the people of Bethel actually interacted with the hippies, they found them polite, respectful, and caring. About the only thing that resembled a crime occurred when kids cut the wire fencing around Max's property and got into the concert without purchasing tickets. But even that wasn't a serious offense, since Mike Lang and I had already announced that the concert was free. And during the concert itself, Woodstock Ventures told the crowd that everyone was welcome.

A true spirit of generosity, sharing, and community took hold of the people at Yasgur's farm. You could see it in their broad smiles, in the peace signs constantly being flashed, and in the helping hands people offered to strangers. Even the difficult conditions did not diminish the festive mood or the love and caring that people showed one another.

Throughout the weekend, heavy downpours occurred periodically, soaking the crowd and turning Max's grassy meadow into one giant field of mud. People had to sit or stand in the mud in order to see the artists as they performed. Even worse, everyone was hungry. Food supplies had become low two weeks before the start of the concert. No one seemed to care. People waited out the rain in their cars, vans, and tents. They shared their food, water, alcohol, and drugs with one another. Happy and festive, people got by with a little help from their friends. Whenever the rain stopped, the music started up again. And wow, what a line-up of artists—Tim Hardin; Melanie; Arlo Guthrie; Joan Baez; Country Joe & the Fish; John Sebastian; Santana; the Grateful Dead; Creedence Clearwater Revival; Janis Joplin; Sly and the Family Stone; The Who; Jefferson Airplane; Joe Cocker; Blood, Sweat, and Tears; Crosby, Stills, Nash, and Young; Sha Na Na; and Jimi Hendrix, among others. The music and lyrics described a beautiful vision of freedom and peace, and the people who came to Woodstock became that vision.

Music filled the entire region. The sound system was so powerful, in fact, that it cleared out every bird in Sullivan County. They didn't come back until after Woodstock was over. For everyone else, the music was a joyful noise.

As for me, the El Monaco Motel was as close to Yasgur's farm as I was going to get. I had a business to run and, thanks to Woodstock, the demands at the El Monaco were overwhelming. Literally thousands upon thousands of people came stumbling onto the El Monaco grounds, needing everything from first aid to water to a place to sleep. My days were a continuous blur of demands—hauling cartons of toilet paper, food, drinks, and bundles of sheets all over the sprawling compound; responding to the frequent screams for help from my mother; and trying to talk hippies down from any number of drug-induced nightmares. Once they came back down to earth, and sanity was restored, most fell asleep right there in the mud. In fact, hundreds of people lay around the El Monaco grounds, stoned, drunk, or snoozing. The place looked like a battlefield after a long siege.

On the Friday that the concert opened, life at the El Monaco made the average circus seem quiet and sedate. No sooner had I finished one job than I had to perform a triple gainer to another. In the midst of all the chaos, I realized that Pop was tired and under the weather. He was bringing some sheets to the Faye Dunaway Wing when I noticed that his face was ashen, exhausted, and more heavily lined than it normally was. I hurried over to him and said, "Here, Pop, give me those sheets. Go take a nap. We're fine here. I'll call you if I need you."

He gave me a tired nod. "Okay, Elli," he said. "Maybe I'll take just a short one."

I spent the rest of the afternoon in the office or in one or another of our buildings, completely absorbed in my work. I was vaguely aware, perhaps, that music was being played somewhere—maybe in the parking lot or on the street. It never pulled me away from what I was doing, though. Then, at about five o'clock that afternoon, the cool shimmer of music reached inside me and drew me back into life. I raised my head from my work and followed the sound to my office window, where I could see people standing in the parking lot and on 17B. They were all looking in the same direction—northwest, toward White Lake. Walking outside, I joined them in the mud. And then I could hear it, as clear and illuminating as sunlight. Richie Havens was singing "Freedom."

Richie's unmistakable voice was rolling down Route 17B like thunder. It bounced over the hills, valleys, and lakes that joined Yasgur's farm and the El Monaco, and when it finally reached us, it lifted us out of our daily concerns and made us believe that all things were possible. I looked off in the direction of Max's farm and smiled. I wasn't able to go to the concert, so the concert had come to me.

The following day started out as crazy as the one before, and got even crazier as the hours went by. Early that Saturday afternoon, just after another downpour, I sat on the motel's front lawn—or what was left of it—and tried to comfort another mud-soaked young man coming down off a bad LSD trip. He was staring off into space, seeing things that weren't there, when I became aware of the sound of a motorcycle roaring down 17B toward the El Monaco. As I turned around, I saw the motorcycle heading directly for us. It came to an abrupt stop just a few feet away, spraying us both with mud. "Are you crazy? This place is full of people. You could have killed someone!" I shouted.

The biker took off her helmet and out fell a long mane of brown hair. She was dressed in a black leather motorcycle jacket and blue denim skirt. Without saying a word, she got off the bike and let the thing drop to the ground. Her face was red and her big eyes suddenly became larger. She stood before me, her mouth slightly open, but she was speechless. She was wet from the rain, and as I looked down, I realized that she was pregnant. Water seemed to be dripping down between her legs, and it clearly wasn't from the rain. *My God,* I thought. *Is that what I think it is?* This woman's water had just broken!

I knew that the situation demanded swift action, yet I also recognized that I was not the best candidate for the job. For starters, I had no idea what to do in a medical emergency. I flunked biology because I wasn't able to slit open my frog for dissection class. I couldn't do heroin—or anything that involved a needle—because I was afraid to puncture my skin. I may look big and burly, but show me where it's written that Mister Big and Burly is able to deliver babies?

The girl's dramatic arrival had brought back to life dozens of drug-addled hippies who, minutes before, had been lying unconscious on the ground. Now they gathered around me, all of them staring aghast at the girl as if she were from another planet. "Wow," one of them said. "She's gonna have a baby."

"Anybody here happen to be a doctor or a nurse?" I asked frantically. They turned their heads and looked at one another. "No" and "Not me, man" were the answers.

"Then at least help me get her into the motel," I shouted. Along with two other men, we formed a seat with our arms and carried the girl into the bar. As the phalanx of men and women slowly moved forward, Papa, baseball bat in hand, rushed over to investigate the commotion. We lay the girl down on the floor, and Pop realized that she was about to give birth.

"Pop, get help!" I ordered. Dumbfounded and disoriented, Pop ran off. I had no idea where he was going.

One of the hippies suddenly got the neurons firing again and said, "I don't think anybody can reach us here, man. Traffic is like stopped."

Holy shit, I realized. *He's right!*

"Somebody call the state police and tell them we have a woman who is about to give birth and we need a doctor here as soon as possible," I told the assembly. "It's the El Monaco Motel," I said. "Tell them we're right on 17B in White Lake."

Several people ran off in different directions. I turned toward the girl and looked into her frightened face—into eyes that were getting bigger by the second. She was maybe twenty years old. When she screamed in pain, her howls cut through my terror and I began functioning.

"You're going to be all right," I said. I looked under her skirt, figuring that was the area to focus on. "I'm going to take off your underwear, okay?" I asked.

A woman, perhaps in her early thirties, sat at the pregnant girl's head. She lifted the girl's head and placed a sweater below it to act as a pillow. The woman began to stroke the girl's hair. "It's going to be all right, baby," she said. "Don't worry, we're here for you." Others sat at her side and offered soothing words of encouragement. People knelt on the floor, surrounding the pregnant woman. I gently removed her panties and remembered, from some TV show, that you're supposed to yell, "Boil some water!" and then

"Push!" What did I know? I didn't have a clue what I might do with boiling water, so I screamed, "Push!"

Relieved that they had something to do, everyone followed my lead and screamed, "Push! Push! Push!"

The pregnant-lady-with-no-name lay on the floor, took a deep breath, screamed heroically, and pushed hard. The older woman at her head kept stroking her and whispering, "You're doing great, honey, you're doing real good. Keep it up."

I vainly screamed "Push" and waited for something to happen. And then something did happen. The top of a dark, hairy head started to emerge from between the girl's legs. I was so excited. A chorus of cheers went up. "You're doing it!" someone yelled. "That's a baby coming out of there," someone else said. "We're going to give birth!" another screamed triumphantly.

I had no idea what to do except to gently support the baby's head as the young woman continued to push.

"Push, push, push, honey, you're almost there," I said. Suddenly, I realized why they call it labor. The poor mother was sweating profusely. She gasped for air and pushed with all her might. *It's hard work to bring a baby into the world,* I thought. It also seemed painful as hell. This little innocent girl with the big eyes and brown hair was pushing with all her might against her body's own resistance. Tissue was tearing, blood was flowing, and tears were streaming down her face. But I could see the fierceness and determination in her eyes.

The chorus suddenly noticed that the baby's head had fully emerged. "It's almost out!" someone yelled. "You're doing it, lady, you're doing it. Keep going. Keep going!"

And then something altogether new happened—a tiny Woodstock baby girl was born into my arms. And it was crying. A huge chorus of cheers went up. "It's a girl!" someone shouted. "Hey, lady, you got a girl! You got a baby girl!"

I was momentarily devoid of all thought. All I could do was marvel. And then I realized that just as the baby was attached to the woman by this long, bloody umbilical cord, I was attached to this woman—even though my attachments to women over the years had been peripheral at best. Blood, guts, and an unclothed mother. It was natural, it was real, and it was such a mess.

I was faced with a dilemma. What should I do with the umbilical cord and whatever it might be attached to? I didn't know. Even a big shot of adrenaline couldn't propel me to cut human tissue. From the crowd of people that surrounded me, someone stepped forward and knelt beside the new mother and child. It was Vilma. She took off her sheer black silk cape and wrapped the child in it.

Someone else bent down and spoke in my ear. "The helicopter is on its way, Elli." That was my father's voice, I realized. He had phoned for help and asked for a helicopter. "They said it would be here in a few minutes." Then he leaned over my shoulder and said, "Boychik, you think you're the only one to get those things to come here?"

I held the baby, still attached to the mother by her cord, and handed her to the mother. I then helped the girl walk outside the bar, all three of us surrounded by about fifty of the baby's newly minted aunts and uncles. Gathering around the front door, we sat down, waiting for the helicopter to arrive. A soft silence overtook us. No one wanted to say a word. It was as if the moment was too special to violate with words. The mother lifted the baby to her breast and began feeding it. Meanwhile, we all rested for what seemed like an eternity.

Finally, I looked at the bedraggled mother and child and naively asked, "How could you, in your advanced condition, come to this festival?"

The new mother looked down at her child, smiled, and then looked back at me. "I didn't know I was this pregnant," she said softly, overcome with happiness. "I never had a kid before."

Suddenly, a state trooper on a great chestnut steed came galloping down 17B and rode up to the motel. He dismounted with a flourish and walked over to our waiting group.

From inside the office of the motel, I saw Momma come running to the center of the commotion.

The state trooper asked me, "Are you the father?"

That's all Momma needed to hear. She cried out, "No! No! Not him! That's mine son. He's not married. He's single, and that girl don't even look Jewish. How could it be him?"

You gotta love the logic, I thought.

"No, I am not the baby's father," I said. "But she needs medical attention fast."

"The helicopter is on its way," the trooper said.

It wasn't long before we heard the soft *whump, whump, whump* of the blades as the helicopter approached the El Monaco. I sat there, reassured by all the memories associated with that familiar sound. I turned to the young mother and said, "Don't worry, the cavalry is on its way." Soon, the great blue and silver whale was hovering above us, scattering articles of clothing and refuse in the wind. The beast descended, touched down softly, and finally settled.

A moment later, the helicopter's door slid open and several people jumped from its hull. An Army doctor in a white coat with a stethoscope in his pocket ran over to the mother and baby.

He put his hand on the mother's shoulder and said, "Ma'am, are you all right?" The young mother nodded yes. "We're going to help you," the doctor told her. He quickly cut the umbilical cord and removed the placenta. *Oy vey,* I thought. *No more cholent for me—ever!*

Two paramedics helped the mother, still holding the baby, onto a stretcher, and swiftly transferred her to the helicopter. The door slid closed and the blades started whirling intensely again. Suddenly, I realized that I didn't even know the mother's name, nor had I asked her what she was going to name her baby.

I backed away and watched the helicopter lift off the ground and rise directly into the sky. It turned southeast and headed toward Manhattan, becoming a dot before disappearing entirely. I smiled and waved good-bye. A sudden and unexpected wave of relief washed over me. I felt lighter, as if a hundred chains that I had carried all my life had fallen in pieces all around me. As the sound of the helicopter's blades faded, the music from Woodstock again rose in my ears.

❦   ❦   ❦

Over the next day and half, the Woodstock concert continued to unfold. Through the intermittent rain and sun, something very special happened. For a moment in history, a nation of young people came together for the joy of sharing music—and, yes, sharing drugs. But there was more. There was an honest-to-God sense of unity, peace, and, above all, love. Four miles away, at the El Monaco, we were no less caught up in this feeling. While there were no more babies to deliver, there was a constant flow of kids freaking out on a multitude of mind-altering substances. And yet for each one who was having a bad trip, there were those compassionate strangers who stopped to help, hold, and talk these young people down from their personal horror shows.

By the time the music came to an end, I was exhausted, physically and emotionally, and yet absolutely elated. I knew that for the first time, I was not alone. The years of hiding my sexuality, being chained to my parents by responsibility, and watching every dollar I made swallowed by a money pit had instilled a deep sense of isolation within me—a feeling of loneliness that never disappeared. But now I felt that I was part of a larger whole, a generation that could define itself by its embracing attitude, its crazy colorful styles, and its love of this new era of rock 'n' roll.

For three glorious days, I was swept up in the social phenomenon that I helped make possible, and the fact that only a few people knew the role I had played wasn't really important. What was important was how I felt. I felt free, and I felt connected to everyone and everything that was around me. Okay, maybe not my mother so much, but with so many of my dreams having come true, I could live with that. We had managed to pay off all the hotel debts, and my mother could now afford to go to Miami Beach in style, along with all the expatriated Catskill clientele. I had finally experienced a few real father-and-son moments. And at that instant, I realized that my future would be as honest, warm, and true as I now knew life could be.

At the end of that summer, after the crowds had finally moved on, we closed up the El Monaco for the season. But in my heart I knew that wherever I went and whatever I did, I'd be taking Woodstock with me. It may not have changed the world, but it had drastically changed my life. And to this day, whenever I see a tie-dyed shirt or hear a song from a Woodstock band, I can't help but smile.

Epilogue

The festival ended on Sunday, August seventeenth. By that time, my old way of life was over. The page had been turned, and returning to New York to resume my work as an art director and interior designer was impossible. What did it matter if one more Park Avenue grande dame had a replica of the Sistine Chapel on her living room ceiling, or if Lord & Taylor had another extravaganza in its Fifth Avenue window?

The values of Woodstock—to insist on the freedom to be oneself and to give and receive love—had transformed me, and there was no going back. On the other hand, I still didn't know how to go forward.

That Monday, exhausted and a bit lost, I sat in my office and watched the long parade of people going home. The police had turned 17B into a three-lane highway moving in only one direction—southeast, toward the New York State Thruway. The exodus was silent and subdued, the crowd spent by the excesses of one very long party. I watched the DayGlo-painted buses, Volkswagen Beetles, pickup trucks, and Harleys motor past my office like a funeral march for a great king. I couldn't watch for long—it felt too much like the lifeblood running out of my veins.

By evening, there was no more traffic. White Lake, Bethel, was a ghost town, eerily silent. That night, Pop, Momma, and I closed up the motel for the season, after which the two of them went to their room and fell asleep. I went to shack number two and did the same—for thirty hours.

Once I regained consciousness, I called Mike Lang and told him that we had about thirty-five thousand dollars in ticket sales that we had to turn over to Woodstock Ventures. Could he come by and pick up the money? I could have sent him a check, of course, but I wanted to see him, if only to connect one more time with the man who had unknowingly changed my life forever.

Mike arrived at the El Monaco, light-hearted and happy. He looked pretty good, considering all that he had been through. Word was out that he was being sued by a whole host of creditors, but, as always, Mike was cool and calm. I knew that he would land on his feet—he had that gift. I mentioned that I was likely to face some trouble from the locals, as well. He told me not to worry—he and his partners would take care of everything before they wrapped up in Bethel.

Before the festival, Mike had informed the town council that he would leave the town in better shape than it was in before Woodstock arrived. As always, his word was gold. He had arranged to keep about three thousand volunteers in Bethel to clean Max's farm and every street in town. The volunteers picked up cans, blankets, clothing, shoes, and much more. By the time they were finished, Bethel fairly glowed.

Mike and I hugged each other and said good-bye. Neither one of us knew at the time that Woodstock would become a cultural icon. It would be twenty years before we saw each other again at a reunion party in Manhattan. We both would appear on several television and radio talk shows to regale listeners with tales of Woodstock. But on that day in the summer of '69, neither of us knew what the future held.

Pop and I spent the next two weeks cleaning up the motel, but when the place was put together again, we both realized that there was nothing left for me in Bethel. I stuffed my clothes and portfolio into my new car—a Cadillac, purchased with some of my Woodstock earnings—closed the trunk, and said good-bye to Pop and Momma.

"You're doing the right thing, Elli," Pop said. "We'll be okay. You'll be okay. If anyone suspicious-looking asks about you, I got one answer—What festival? Who's Elliot Tiber? I'm Jack Teichberg. I never saw no festival. *Gei gezunta hei, son.* (Yiddish for "Go in good health.") I'm proud of you."

Two weeks later, I was in Hollywood, California. There, I was admitted to the movie set design union, which I hoped would lead to a career in film. But fate had other plans. Eight months later, in May 1970, one of my sisters called and told me that my father had been hospitalized with colon cancer. The doctors didn't expect him to live long.

I raced to Bethel and found Pop in the Monticello hospital, lying in an oxygen tent, barely conscious. For the next few weeks, I made regular trips to his bedside. Most of our time together was spent in silence, with me holding his hand. But one day in early June, when I was about to get up to leave, I felt his hand suddenly grasp mine with surprising strength. I moved my head closer to the plastic tent to catch his whisper.

"My little boy, my son," he began. "I love you. I know about you. I know what you do. I know about your life, your friends. I just want you should know it's okay by me. I hope you find somebody and you can be happy." He looked deeply into my eyes and nodded his approval and love. He paused before starting again. "I have just one thing to ask you. When I go, I want to be buried facing Woodstock. You know that little Jewish cemetery just near Max's farm? That's where I want to be. The festival was the best time of my whole life, and you did it."

"No, Pop," I replied. "We did it. You and me."

In the silence that followed, I found the question that, on so many occasions, had begged for an answer. "Pop," I said. "Why did you stay with Momma all these years? You were so tired. Why didn't you ever tell her to stop her demands?"

"I love her," he whispered. Those were the last words I heard him speak. The next day he was dead.

When I gave Momma the news of Pop's death, she had a shrieking fit. "Yankl, how could you do this to me?" she wailed. "How could you leave me here alone at the beginning of the season? How will I manage? How will I rent the rooms and make the beds and mow the lawns by myself? How could you leave me alone in the motel for Decoration Day? Who will fix the plumbing? You never gave me one good day in mine life! Not one moment of happiness! Never! You never gave me one good day in mine whole life!"

We buried Pop in the cemetery that overlooked Max's farm. That same year, a family that owned Italian restaurants in the

Bronx bought the El Monaco and turned it into yet another Italian restaurant. We sold most of our belongings and I installed Momma in a posh Jewish senior citizen's home in Riverdale, New York. There was a synagogue on the premises, along with a rabbi and plenty of yentas with whom she could gossip. Once she settled in, she told me that she was happy. "It's wonderful here," she said one day. "*Unzereh menschen,*" she said. ("Our people.")

As it turned out, she never had to face one of her greatest fears—growing old without enough money in her purse. Some time after I placed her in the retirement home, I learned that over the years, she had managed to squirrel away about one hundred thousand dollars in cash from motel receipts—money that neither Pop nor I ever knew about.

In the early 1990s, Momma died, having spent virtually all the money she had saved for her retirement. Just before she passed, I told her that I was writing a book about Woodstock and the exciting adventure we had shared at the El Monaco.

"I hope you don't mention my name in your book," she said. "Don't tell people where I am. What would I say if reporters asked me what went on? I would better shut up and not tell them nothing, since I don't want to ruin your book. I hated all those kids with their dirty sex and drugs—kids who should be home with their mothers. I hated the music, too. I was ashamed you were there. I don't know why you are reminding people who you were and where you are now. They will blame you because you were the one who made that Woodstock happen. I am ashamed of you and Woodstock."

Some things never change.

None of that mattered to me anymore because I had found the single thing I had spent my life looking for—love. In the spring of

1971, I met Andre Ernotte, a Belgian director and professor who was in Manhattan on a Harkness Fellowship to study American theater. Andre was in his early thirties, tall—about six feet two—handsome, and lean. In all my life, I had never met anyone with whom I could so easily talk and share myself as I could with Andre.

Three months after we met, Andre went back to Belgium, and I soon followed. There in Brussels, the two of us made a home. The European temperament suited my sensibilities, and my creativity blossomed. I learned French and wrote for television, theater, and film. Later I became the dramaturge of the National Theater of Belgium. Andre and I collaborated on many screenplays and theater productions, not only in Belgium, but also in France and other European countries.

In the mid-1970s, I wrote a book, *Rue Haute,* about the Nazi occupation of Brussels during World War II. The book became a bestseller in Europe and was translated into English and published by Avon books in the United States as *High Street.* Andre and I collaborated on the screenplay, which was made into a film by the same name and distributed in the U.S. The film, which won numerous awards in both Europe and the States, was hailed by *The New York Times* as an extraordinary tour de force. As with so many of our collaborations, Andre directed the picture.

Andre's and my love made it possible to work together in all areas of life—from cooking and planning an ordinary day, to writing, producing, and directing a major play or motion picture. When one of us had to travel on business, we wrote love letters and poetry to each other—Andre's always in the most exquisite French and English.

In 1999, Andre became ill and eventually died of cancer. We had been together for twenty-eight years. After his death, I moved back to New York, where I became a professor of comedy writing and performance at both the New School University and Hunter College.

In October 2006, I was invited to Beverly Hills for the Academy of Motion Picture Arts and Sciences' thirty-sixth anniversary of the film *Woodstock*. At the reunion, I saw many of my old Woodstock friends, including Mike Lang, Stan Goldstein, and Joel Rosenman. We marveled at how we all had changed. In fact, we had all simply grown up.

There's an old saying that the journey is more important than the destination. The summer of '69 taught me the truth of that statement. Somehow, Stonewall and Woodstock stirred some crazy alchemy inside me so that the many separate strands of my being blended together and became one man. That crazy mix made possible all my dreams, including the most important dream of all, my life partner, Andre Ernotte.

And now, several decades after Woodstock, I can lean back and feel the satisfaction of the journey. I have climbed the mountain— at least the one that was placed before me. And like my old nemesis, Moses, I found something important at its peak. In my case, though, it wasn't some heavy set of laws. It was the music that helped define my life.